Angela Goode was born in Adelaide in 1948. She was educated at Girton School, studied at the SA School of Art and completed a Bachelor of Arts degree at Latrobe University in 1976, majoring in Sociology. She is married with four children.

Having worked as a radio copywriter, television presenter and freelance radio journalist, she joined *The Advertiser* in Adelaide as a general reporter and feature writer in 1978.

In 1981, after marrying a cattleman and moving to the country, she began her popular column about rural life and farming 'The Goode Life', which is published in *The Advertiser* and *The Weekly Times*, in Victoria.

Since 1988, she has presented a weekly segment of the same name for the South Australian 'Country Hour' on ABC radio. *Great Working Dog Stories* had its genesis in one of these segments.

Mike Hayes claims his Mum always preferred dogs to people. That's why he was eight years old before he received his first distemper shot. On the other hand, the family's pets went to all the best schools and did exceptionally well as quantity surveyors, politicians and BMW owners. He was reduced to having to write for a living first as a journalist, then as a broadcaster, film maker and author.

The cruel irony of it all is that some of the most popular stories during ten years of writing about the Prickle Farm for the ABC and hundreds of similar stories for newspapers and magazines, have been about dogs.

Mike Hayes is almost house trained, is good with children but can't be trusted around cats or lambing ewes.

Farewell to the
    Harter family.

It has been a delight
knowing you.

May God bless you as you
return home & continue
your walk with Him.

Fond regards from
Ian & Mack Lockwood

P.B.C.   17. 7. 94

1 Cor 15: 58

GREAT WORKING DOG STORIES

Angela Goode

Mike Hayes

an
ABC
BOOK

Published by ABC Books for the
AUSTRALIAN BROADCASTING CORPORATION
GPO Box 9994 Sydney NSW 2001

Copyright © Angela Goode, Mike Hayes, 1990

First published August, 1990
Reprinted September 1990
Reprinted January 1991
Reprinted July 1991
Reprinted October 1992
Reprinted December 1992
Reprinted February 1993
Reprinted July 1993

National Library of Australia
Cataloguing-in-Publication entry
Great working dog stories.
  ISBN 0 7333 0044 8.
  1. Working dogs—Australia—Anecdotes.
  I. Hayes, Mike. II. Goode, Angela.
  III. South Australian Country hour
  (Radio program).
636.73

Illustrated by Angela Goode
Edited by Jo Jarrah
Designed by Helen Semmler
Set in 10/12pt Schneidler Old Style Light
by Midland Typesetters, Victoria
Printed and bound in Australia by
Australian Print Group, Victoria

7-2-2-2-3-3-2-3-1495
12 11 10

The publishers wish to acknowledge the assistance
of the makers of MEATY BITES Working Dog Formula

FOREWORD

Country dogs are a breed apart. They mightn't look like anything special, yet they are the greatest of the nation's workers. Uncomplaining, tough, unfussed over, you'll never find a more faithful bunch. Rarely will they go on strike, and they'll always do their best to please. They are our unsung heroes.

For over 200 years they have barked at the heels of our livestock or eyed it into submission, often doing the work of two humans. And work . . . once they're off their chains or out of their kennels, they'll work anything, no matter what the weather or the time of day. From cracker ewes to stud bulls, they're not fussy. They'll also stalk the chooks, round up children and mesmerise the budgies. They are the original workaholics.

They'll rarely win prizes for beauty, even though many are blessed with fancy pedigrees. They often bear the scars of toil and fights—ripped ears, crooked tails, missing clumps of hair, even missing legs. Nor are they strong on social skills. Head through the local town with a ute-load of dogs, and you'll need ear muffs. Every opposition ute with a dog is a rival to be abused with all force. For a dog's ute is his personal territory to be defended at all times.

At the local shop, they pile out and stake their claim on every tyre and post. If another team of workers pulls in the staking of territory gets more frantic. Hackles rise, bodies circle each other and the lips retract in fearsome snarls. A whistle from each respective boss quells the looming war and sends the teams back to the safety of their home bases from where they bark open abuse again.

They adorn their utes like figureheads, riding atop bales of hay with their eyes blown to slits and pink strap tongues tugging in the wind. Or they're a restless, yapping scrum rushing from side to side on the tray top. No farm ute looks properly dressed without a working dog on board.

Working dogs obey orders promptly otherwise they are unlikely to survive for long. Give them the signal and they're up on the motorbike with the boss heading for work, one fore and one aft, hanging on with their toes and riding the swerves like Hell's Angels.

In the paddock, they are all lean concentration, with one eye on the boss and the other on the stock. The eye dogs will stick their rumps in the air and creep forward on their elbows with heads low to the ground, controlling the mob with finesse, grace and slightly bulbous eyes. The young dogs will rush and bark and send animals in all directions. From across the peaceful paddocks you might hear raised voices and shouts of 'Sit', 'Sit', as the boss attempts to curb an exuberant performance. The language can get a lot more colourful.

A working dog is a versatile creature, but never is this more apparent than when a car-load of city visitors arrives at a farm. Farm dogs recognise that a clean, shiny car and clean, shiny children are a soft touch. They know better than to turn on the charm for the occupants of a dirty country vehicle because farmers are immune to their leering smiles and weaving, wagging bodies.

City cars are part of a canine cargo cult bringing free love from an alien world. This is the world where one can lavish people with slobbery kisses and muddy paws and get pats, cuddles and even a few jellybeans in return. And the lads drop their eyelids in demure ecstacy as they get their ears scratched. The visitor for the duration of the visit finds a head with a pair of pleading eyes shoved up for scratching at every opportunity. . .until finally the pests are banished to their kennels.

A farm dog, if he is any good, is a treasure. His boss will defend his honour hotly. The trouble is every bloke reckons his dog's better than the next bloke's.

In October 1988, on the South Australian Country Hour, we decided that, as a tribute to Australian working dogs, we would run a competition to unearth some of their great unheralded feats. We were not necessarily looking for the greatest working dog of all time, but trying to capture the essence of what working dogs mean to people on the land.

The entries were so colourful, so varied and so readable that many form the core of this book. They reveal the great respect farmers have for their dogs, how dependent they are on them and how deep a working relationship forged over many years can become. There are tales of intuitive dogs, heroic dogs and dogs that sit in the ute watching others work. There are hilarious stories, sad stories, and studies of canine characters. The stories also give a special insight into Australian rural life, past and present.

In all, I have tried to preserve the expression and style of each writer. This extends to retaining imperial measures as is generally the rural habit.

A selection of these stories was read on ABC radio by Country Hour presenter Peter Knudsen, past NFF president and now MHR, Ian McLachlan, and me.

For allowing me to stage the competition, I thank Ian Doyle, Peter Knudsen and the South Australian Country Hour staff, and for their wonderful enthusiasm and ready assistance.

I also thank Dalgety Bennetts Farmers for the prize of a year's supply of Skippa working dog formula which was awarded to Bruce Mills of Tumby Bay for his entry about Spike ('He found his own mob').

Contributors of other stories collected during my travels around South Australia are also thanked for breaking off their chores to give me their time.

Finally, I pay respect to Lucy, my border collie who left the city with me to joyfully spend the last six years of her life among the bush sights, smells and sounds that her genes told her were the only ones that mattered.

Angela Goode

A BIT FURTHER FOREWORD

Near where we live at Laggan, in southern New South Wales, there's an old flour mill which in recent years has been transformed into a trendy restaurant. Graham Liney, the bloke responsible for it all, has a great feeling for history and has collected a swag of local relics. Pride of place is taken by a large photograph of his mill, taken sometime in the 1880s. It must have been quite an occasion for the locals. Several of them turned out in their best clobber, with the hairy clumper horses all scrubbed up, to pose for the photographer. Who knows? It was probably the first experience any of them had had of a shutterbug. Those bygone citizens are pictured astride their horses, full of dignity and decorum.

In the same photo are four local dogs. Close examination shows two of them fidgeting with their most intimate parts, one dragging his itchy bum over the gravel and the fourth halfway through what is undoubtedly a monster poop. The old photo tells it all.

While mankind felt duty-bound to celebrate the occasion with pomposity and self-importance, the dogs marked their millisecond in history as only they could. I'm no expert on animal behaviour, but it seems to me those scrubby canines are exhibiting for posterity their most outstanding attribute. I firmly believe that, apart from a sadly dwindling number of humans, dogs are the only form of life that clearly exhibit a sense of humour.

In a book like this, it's easy and somewhat obvious to write about their nobility, their intelligence and their loyalty. But all the dogs I've known stand out in my memory because of that unique ability to look back at you over their shoulder, in a moment of total disaster, with what's undoubtedly the cheekiest grin in the world.

My dog memories, and therefore my dog stories, aren't all sweetness and light. I've tried to tell these yarns as they happened. You might notice that I haven't necessarily stuck to correct names, precise dates and carefully researched locations . . . but the stories are fair dinkum. The names and places—those trappings of humankind—don't really matter all that much. They're secondary to the real heroes whose contribution to recorded history, quite rightly, is registered in terms of an itchy posterior.

Mike Hayes

CONTENTS

FARMING CHANGES, BUT DOGS NEVER DO

John P. Pickering, Pt Noarlunga

Uncle Charlie had some dogs round 50 years ago,
Times were tough, the Depression on and horses were the go,
Drays and jinkers, sulkies too and wagons and the like,
And dust storms as you've never seen, they just cut out the
    light.
The farm dog's life was very rough, they really lived quite
    hard,
No nice soft bed inside, you see, but tethered in the yard.
They ate quite well, as meat goes off and soon begins to smell,
With no refrigeration and flies and heat as well.

The roo dog's job was rabbits, he really did quite swell,
But not quite good enough—they had a poison cart as well,
It dropped bran and phosphorous bait behind a tired old horse,
It killed nearly everything and native birds of course.
The staghound's job was foxes, but the story was the same,
Sheepguts behind the sulky, strychnine poison, quarter grain.
The sheepdog was my favourite, one night got off the chain.
He ate just one fox bait—not seen alive again.

Those dogs were workers then, you see, and farmers were the
    same,
They started well before the dawn, like dogs, did not complain.
They worked in rain and sun and hail, they cleared, they burned,
    they logged,
Wherever Uncle Charlie was the dogs behind him jogged.
I don't think dogs are different, we have altered now some-
how.
Agriculture is big business with its brawls, fights and row.
Uncle Charlie's breed died out and has now been replaced,
By another breed of farmer—I think he'd feel disgraced.

Cheap loans and grants, concessions and the like,
Old uncle didn't know a thing about the interest hike.
There was no money borrowed then, things were made not
  bought,
Bread was baked, and butter made and metal things were
  wrought.
The 'waste not, want not' theory was worked to a fine art,
Many's the time the junk heap would yield up that spare part.
People seemed so happy then, life a slower pace.
Now—buy, borrow and before you pay, replace.

Digressing as I am from dogs, they really are the same,
No interest in the price of wool or in the futures game,
Whether in the country or whether in the town,
They are the one thing you can rely on when the chips are
  down.

XV

PART 1

COCKCROW

It all begins with a pup (though Minus prefers kittens) and then the training–or trouble–starts. It seems some are born to it, some come good eventually (even at ten!) and others–well . . .

BORN AT THE DRAFTING GATES

Ian Jackson, Tirlta Station, Broken Hill

The September shearing was approaching at Rowena Station and Spike, the two-tan kelpie bitch, sits by my side in the shed awaiting the arrival of the sheep from the outstation. Yard and shed work is her specialty. She doesn't like paddock work.

It was with horror that I realised that at this, the busiest time of the year, just as the annual harvest of the fleeces was about to commence, I was about to lose my right hand 'man'. Spike's belly swelled in tandem with the increase in her work load. Shearing progressed steadily, but I knew that at any time she would have to give up her job to deliver her pups.

I couldn't understand how she could always be at my side when there was yard work to be done. I knew she was a totally dedicated working dog, but I was nevertheless surprised, considering the advanced state of her pregnancy. One Wednesday, she was really struggling to help us draft 2000 sheep. I had to rescue her several times from the top of the yard fences where she had been caught in limbo. Her love of sheep meant that she wouldn't leave the shed, even at night. I felt abandoned when I drove the 12 miles home without her, but she wouldn't come.

On Thursday morning, I went mustering to bring in 500 ewes for the afternoon run. I was by myself and as I was pushing the sheep up into the drafting race, Spike rushed up, bounding over the fences, smiling and happy, obviously trying to tell me she had delivered the pups.

She had delivered them right at the foot of the drafting gates where I usually stand. They were minute, fresh pups, the whole seven of them. I relocated them at the beginning of the race, so they could still feel involved.

I drafted the ewes with Spike's help before she returned to the pups and I had to leave for Tirlta Station.

That evening, my brother, who had come up from South Australia to help during shearing, much needed when the best dog is out of action, asked me if I had seen the new pups. I said I had seen her seven little beauties and that she had helped me draft the ewes. My brother said she had also helped him draft sheep, but that she now had ten pups.

It seems that she had produced another three after helping me a few hours earlier.

Four weeks later, she suffered a severe case of milk fever and nearly died. Too much hard work as well as the caring of her pups was to blame. We organised an emergency flight to Broken Hill where she was treated by the local vet on the airport lawns. He saved her life.

A few days later, she was back in the yards and shed. All pups are healthy and strong. One of the male pups looks like being a champion—like his mother.

THE GOANNA

Barry Smith, Cowell

It was late December, about 1940, when my uncle, his workman and my cousin who was about ten years old, headed out in the truck to load bags of wheat. My cousin, being a real farm boy, had with him a young sheepdog about six months old.

As soon as they arrived in the paddock, the boy and the pup started exploring. Within a very short time, my uncle heard the pup start a continual yap as young dogs do when chasing something they are not able to catch.

Upon casting his eye around, my uncle (who was loading

3

the bags from the ground) spotted the pup chasing a goanna about three to four feet long. The sight of the goanna up on all four legs speeding through the stubble with the yapping pup right behind was, at the least, very entertaining—until the goanna decided to head for safety. There being no trees in sight, my uncle represented the only chance for the goanna to climb to safety from the pup.

All of a sudden, uncle saw the large goanna speeding straight towards him. Panic set in and he turned and fled.

After a few quick paces out into the paddock and a glance over his shoulder, he saw a rapidly gaining, frightened goanna. A second glance, and with presence of mind, uncle jumped into the air with legs wide apart. The speeding goanna zoomed through. Uncle landed and, with a great sigh of relief, watched as the speeding goanna ran off.

After only a few yards, though, it did a wheelie and sped back to an astonished uncle who took to his heels for the truck. With a quick glance, he calculated he was not going to make it. So he did a second jump, and the goanna sped through towards the truck, wheeled around and came back again.

By this time, on a hot day, uncle was becoming alarmed and exhausted. As the goanna came back for try number three, uncle made sure he did not run as fast and end up too far from the truck. With a calculated third jump and evasion as soon as the frightened reptile shot through, uncle spun around and headed for the truck.

As his build was somewhat short and stocky, the height of the truck tray appeared enormous. Uncle hit it with a thud and managed to roll on just as the speeding goanna and pup shot through.

A very red-faced, exhausted, and slightly irritated farmer turned upon his workman (who by this stage was rolling around on the tray splitting his sides with laughter) and roared, 'Why didn't you call that . . . pup off?'

Eventually he managed to squeeze out—'I couldn't'.

MINUS PLUS FOUR

Lorna Schwarz, Ceduna

Our dog, Minus, was born with her left leg missing. There was just a stump where her leg should have been.

She was one of a litter of six and predictably the poor little pup with the stump won the hearts of the children. We thought she should have been put down.

Minus thrived and, despite her handicap, could almost keep up to the other dogs. In the paddock and the yards, she was just as competent and able.

We were terribly surprised one day to discover that Minus had adopted four small kittens. They were actually suckling from her, and getting milk, despite the fact that Minus had never had pups.

These kittens, whose mother had either abandoned them or died, grew and were constant companions to Minus. They followed her everywhere, constantly.

One day, a neighbour found Minus and her family out on our main road about four kilometres from home—just out walking!

They were an extraordinary sight.

Minus was well-known by all the folk around here, so they were brought home.

RUNNING BACKWARDS

Kath Alcock, Naracoorte

Digger was my dog. By this I mean that he stayed by me, whereas other dogs which I handled and 'broke in' clung to the boss.

He was an odd-looking dog, large heavy body and rather spindly legs, mostly black, with white under the neck and on his toe tips. His mother was a border collie, moderately long-haired, and I suspect his sire was a short-haired border collie whose ancestry, I was told by the neighbouring owner, included a very intelligent Scotch collie. This, I believe, is where Digger's odd body shape came from.

At about four months, he obediently came when whistled and sat when ordered to, but as for showing any inclination to work sheep, he was just a wood-head!

We had a small flock of very quiet stud sheep, and Digger commenced his training on these. I believe that sheepdogs should always be trained whilst the owner is on foot. Then he should graduate to a horse and lastly, to a vehicle.

At the start, he was only interested in scooping up the droppings of the very new lambs. But I persisted until one day he suddenly realised what he was on this earth for, and went ahead in leaps and bounds. As he progressed, he did a lot of thinking for himself, but wasn't headstrong at all.

One time, I drove the car down the paddock with Digger racing enthusiastically ahead, until we came to the point of rounding up the sheep. When we had them in one mob, I got back into the car and we moved off in the right direction.

There always will be those cunning and wily ewes which break off at a tangent and rapidly lead the rest of the mob away. This is just what happened. There was a lot of confusion with ewes and lambs veering off in two directions, and a few keeping to the correct path. So I got out of the vehicle and rounded them up again and instructed Digger to 'wing' each side back and forth, which he quickly learned. We got to the gate and then to the sheepyards with no further trouble. Drafting sheep with Digger was a breeze and whenever I gave him praise, he smiled with his eyes and wagged his tail. He truly loved the learning process.

He was an eager learner and had only to be shown a new order the one time. He even learned to shut the houseyard gate which I opened and deliberately left that way as I passed through. Dig got behind the gate and put both front paws on the mesh and gave it a vigorous shove until it crashed into position.

He knew not to come into the houseyard until invited and would lie with his nose in line with the fence if the gate happened to be open and there were no chooks around.

If I was working in the orchard, and he was off the chain, he would sneak between the shed and the garden fence, hop over a low part and, trying to make himself small, would creep up to me.

'What are you doing here?' I'd say, and those loving eyes would just about melt a rock.

One day we were out walking in the pine plantation. It was late spring and a fairly warm day. Suddenly, from the corner of my eye, I noticed Digger prop in his stride and saw, about a metre in front of him, a big brown snake. Its head was upraised. I think this was more in warning, than a sign it was about to strike.

'No Dig!' I yelled. I can still picture that tableau—the snake and dog, rigidly eyeing each other. Digger was on three backward slanting legs and one forepaw was up and bent at the knee. At the fear in my shout, he 'ran' backwards for several paces! I had never seen any dog do that before. The snake slid under a heap of pine slash in fluid motion.

WEE TROUBLES

Sue Hood, Naracoorte

Gus wasn't the best-looking pup, but we were told he had plenty of potential. He was always a little too frisky with the children and the wonder dog was never that wonderful with the sheep. We loved him though—that is, until he developed this disgusting habit of urinating on people whenever they patted him on the back.

We were horrified, but soon got wise to his insulting behaviour and would shun him on opening the back door. No-one ever tied him up at night, just in case he let fly. He was always left to the master of the house.

It happened that my husband had to go away for the night. So, for convenience, I tied Gus to an old post in the garden.

During the night, a storm blew up. Gus, on his post, started whining and barking. I tried to shut it out by putting my head under the pillow, but the noise got worse.

Eventually, in nightie, parka and rubber boots, I went out into the storm. The dog's chain was wound around the post very tightly and he was choking. I proceeded to untangle him when, inadvertently, I touched his back. Over he rolled and urinated all over me.

He is now dead, and I miss him not a bit.

THE PUPPY IN THE DUST

Rachel Biven, Beaumont

Around twelve years ago, my son Peter went to Esperance in Western Australia. After working at odd jobs on various farms, he obtained a 3000 acre block which he and his Danish wife, Kirsten, were developing.

Peter and Kirsten had leased some grain-cleaning works to help them finance the work on the block.

It was a busy time for them as huge loads of grain would arrive in road trains to be cleaned and pickled. My husband and I were visiting them to give them a hand. My husband helped maintain the noisy 'Heath Robinson' machinery. I helped sew up bags of grain while Kirsten flipped them from the trolley onto a pile.

One day, Peter found a little black puppy amongst the dust and dirty, empty bags. Above the noisy machinery, he roared 'Get this thing out of here.'

Kirsten and I felt motherly, and between jobs we managed to pet it and feed it.

The day ended, and Peter said firmly, 'We don't want any more animals to feed.' They already had three stray cats and his working dog, Ben. The pathetic-looking pup was left in the shed and ignored in the hope that a truck driver who may have left it behind would reclaim it.

Next morning, the puppy was still there. But suddenly there was a drama as it was noticed that Ben was looking very sick. Peter recognised the signs of poisoning and immediately dropped everything and rushed the dog to the vet. He was too late to save him, despite drips and injections.

Gradually, the puppy soothed our sad hearts. Ben had been a great friend and worker.

The little pup sensed she must win Peter's affection. She sat watching him with her big, black eyes, trying to charm the man of the house. She licked him and watched his every move. She sat at his feet, with her little white, dainty paws crossed.

Instead of continually trying to give her away to everyone who came to the shed, Peter finally gave her a name—Molly.

Harvest time came out on the block, 130 kilometres out into the bush. The convoy of caravans, tractors, harvesters, a water tank and the utility, with Molly firmly sitting on the loaded back, finally got away.

Molly was happy at the block, darting around barking at birds and lizards. When she killed a brown snake in the bush shower, she was suddenly a heroine. Her efforts at sheep work were, nevertheless, scorned after the well-trained Ben. No-one, of course, expected her to be any good. She was just a whippet-border collie cross.

Molly, however, gradually wormed her way firmly into her family's hearts. She danced on her hind legs and popped balloons with her teeth at Christmas. She grovelled at Peter's feet, she smiled and made people laugh and finally, they even let her sleep on their bed when winter came.

Shearing time came around and we were all trying to push sheep into the yards. Pete was still without a working dog. Suddenly, Molly came bouncing into the yards. She yapped, nipped the heels of the ewes, and leapt onto their backs. Expertly, she pushed those sheep into the yards and we were able to pen up without any trouble. She learnt to pull a ration sheep down, and eventually became everything a working dog should be.

She was petted and loved, minded the children and still 'made eyes' at Peter.

She had pups every year and everyone wanted them.

Rabbits were bad one year so the Council spread 1080 poison. Molly got a dose and was terribly ill. After three days at the veterinary hospital on drips she returned to carry on her duties.

Some years later, we returned to see Peter and Kirsten's new baby. There was Molly, sitting beside the bassinet with her white paws crossed, watching and keeping alert. When the baby cried, she would run off and tug at Kirsten's jeans. Then, when she heard the utility, she would leap on to the tray, yapping and wanting to help with the sheep—pleased to leave her women's work behind.

The neighbour at the farm next door often went spotlighting for rabbits and foxes. One night, Molly must have been out chasing rabbits herself, and she returned next morning bleeding and hurt. We found that a bullet had gone right through her collar and neck and passed out the other side. Apart from the hole and wound, she was uninjured.

She was an extraordinary, versatile dog and she had an amazing capacity for survival.

A CAR FULL OF GOATS

Mrs Noel Greatz, Renmark

After a heavy rain, my husband decided to drive out to the far corner of the property to check the catchment of water in the dams.

As usual in the bush, when Dad went in the car, Mum, kids and an assortment of dogs went too. Our mode of transport was an elderly Holden sedan minus the boot-lid—removed so we could stand in the back while spotlighting.

On this particular day, we had only one 'worthy' sheepdog, a border collie named Trixie, as well as a small Heinz housedog and a six-month-old red kelpie, Tip.

About four miles from home, we came upon a small mob of eight wild goats on a grassy plain. Being a bit sceptical about the red kelpie ever making a good sheepdog, I suggested to my husband that we put the dogs around the goats to test Tip's mustering ability.

Away they went, including the housedog, chasing the mob of goats away from us. Suddenly all our scoffing stopped as the mob changed direction and headed straight for our car. Soon the goats were milling around us as we stood by the car bursting with laughter. Then one very pregnant nanny

11

jumped into the back seat and refused to move. The rest took refuge in the boot of the car. We couldn't believe our eyes, and regret not having a camera.

The dogs were racing in circles around the vehicle screaming about how clever they were. But our big problem was how to get rid of them out of the car. All seven goats lay down and refused to budge. Yelling with excitement, the children suggested Dad drive off at full speed (20 mph in soft ground) and then perhaps the goats would jump out with fright. They didn't. They clung on for dear life. After about a mile of wheelies, we had to stop and physically lift every damned goat out, including the fat nanny who was sitting with the children on the back seat. Tip grew up to be an excellent sheepdog.

CITY SLICKER

C. Bryce, Yankalilla

As a boy, I spent most of my spare time wandering the different places in the bush where we lived. I walked the hills of the Barossa, explored the wide flat country of Keith and trekked through the sandhills near Robe. Always by my side was my mate, Skeet.

His mother was a stray who was caught killing sheep. She was about to be shot when it was noticed she was heavily pregnant. We let her have the pups and Skeet was the one we kept. He wasn't very handsome, but I didn't care. He made up for his lack of looks by learning everything I taught him. He would sit until I told him to move, sometimes for half an hour. He would bark, fetch balls, jump, come, go and I think he even tried to speak. Anyway, we were great mates.

Sometimes when it was very cold, I'd even sneak him inside and let him sleep on my bed. Mum never found out because he had learned to tiptoe silently.

Eventually, I went off to ag. college. Dad had died so Mum moved to the city. She looked after him for me and he gave her company and barked at strangers.

When I finished my three-year course, I went off to be a jackeroo in the station country down south. They were running 20,000 merinos and I was one of twelve jackeroos. Every bloke had to have a dog, and some of the big shots had two. We were heavily into proving our manhood and a couple of dogs in the back of the ute was better than one.

Every morning, we would all assemble by the quarters to get our day's jobs from the boss. Actually, most of the time, we couldn't even hear him because if you can imagine twelve blokes all with at least one dog and the boss with his dog—our morning briefings were usually just one big dogfight.

The boss's dog was the worst. I mean, his dog seemed to know he was the top dog, so to speak. He would go around picking on all the other dogs, just giving them a nip or a push in a sneaky, thuggish sort of way. We couldn't do anything much about it because, well, we were just the underlings. When one of our dogs did snarl in retaliation, though, the boss's kelpie would hurl himself at him and fight until the other was a bloody mess. He was a dirty fighter.

The boss would pretend he didn't even notice. He would just drone on as though nothing was happening—even though the rolling, screaming bodies might have been right at his feet. I think he liked seeing other blokes' dogs beaten up. And you didn't dare try to rescue your dog either, because that would mean you thought yours was a bit of a sis or something. All you could do was to kick the boss's dog when the boss wasn't looking, or chuck rocks at him out in the paddock. I did that once and he yelped and limped for ages. The boss thought he had been kicked by a cow.

Anyway, with Mum widowed and not much money to go around among the eight of us, I couldn't think of getting a fancy sheepdog for myself. Skeet was all I had. Besides, I loved the old bugger. He had never seen sheep close-up because we only had cattle or crops on our places. But he had a bit of

13

working dog in him, and better than that, he was a bloody good fighter. I knew that if anyone laughed at his funny-shaped body or tatty ears, I could set him on his dog. There's no greater crime in the bush than criticising a bloke's dog. You can say his wife's ugly but you can't laugh at his dog. People have been shot for that.

So, I rolled up with my old mate sitting beside me in my ute. He would have been offended if I had put him in the back. He peered down his scarred old nose at all the mutts that came out from under the jackeroos' quarters to bark at us, and when he alighted, he regally peed on the wheel of my ute, surveyed the milling throng and trotted stiffly, with his head in the air and his hackles bristling slightly, with me to my room. He slept on my bed and accepted his change of address without any fuss.

At the briefing next morning, Skeet sat beside me, surveying the morning dogfights with disdain. When the boss's thug walked up to check him out, Skeet's old lips curled, his hackles rose and he let out a fearsome, gravelly growl. The thug froze, and retreated. I patted the ugly old bugger's head, but he probably didn't know he'd done anything special.

For a few months, I didn't get much sheep work. The blokes with proven dogs got most of the yard work and mustering, and although Skeet was doing all right with the cattle and enjoyed following my horse all day, no-one had much time for him.

I did get my turn eventually. Now I don't know if old Skeet had been watching what the top dogs had been doing, but he worked in the yards like he'd been doing it all his life. Look, he was basically a city dog. He knew about roads and traffic and chasing cats, but here he was leaping rails, speaking up, backing sheep, forcing and staying back just like the best of them. I felt my chest was bursting with pride. And although the old fellow was ten when he worked his first sheep, he never let up even if it was stinking hot or pelting with rain.

Later on, he moved with me to Western Australia and if I hadn't had such a good dog, I wouldn't have got the good jobs I did. In time, old Skeet sired Louie with the cooperation of some station hussy . . . and this dog of even less breeding surpassed even his great old dad as a worker. Which all goes to show that pedigrees haven't got a lot to do with talent.

14

TAKE A DOG

Jill Dobbs, Port Augusta

The working dogs in my life are, to a man, male chauvinist pigs.

My husband owns three sheepdogs—one old, one not so old and one quite young. They are fawningly devoted to him, and except for the odd inexplicable occasion, they do most things he requires of them in most situations.

They are devoted to me too—and so they should be. In each case it was me who was left with the eight-week-old, sleepy bundle of fur at the end of its first day here. Admiration time over, the boss would yawn and stretch and say, in his lordly way, 'I'm for bed. You'll fix him up, won't you?'

In each case it was me who converted a carton into a snug puppy nest with an old boss-smelling pullover. It was me who crept out in the cold night in response to the whimpers of the occupant. It was me who dispensed comforting saucers of milk and me who mopped up afterwards.

It was me who attended to wormings, vaccinations, diet and pest control. As the dogs grew older, it was me who nursed them through ailments and injuries ranging in severity from bee-stung nose to fractured pelvis. To this day, it is me who feeds and waters them and ties them up at sundown, and when the boss is away, or engaged in dogless work, it is me who lets them off for exercise.

They reward me with effusive displays of affection, to which I respond with enthusiasm, but will they work for me? Never.

'If you'll just load the last of those rams in the ute and take them to the ewes,' says the boss, poised to do something else, 'I'll leave a dog to help you get them up the ramp.'

Does A Dog do anything of the sort? Not he! When asked, cajoled, ordered, and finally yelled at, he simply remains at my side, tail slightly wagging and eyes fixed on my face.

'What's she on about?' his expression plainly says. 'She only ever calls me to come and be fed, or chained, or dosed or fussed

15

over, and here I am, obediently at her side, waiting for any one of those things to happen. 'Surely, she can't be expecting me to do anything about these sheep. That's work for the boss and me—not her and me.'

Eventually, A Dog tires of looking at my face and it goes and lies in the shade of the ramp while I struggle on alone, manhandling every unwilling ram up the ramp and into the stock crate.

Another time, with another dog, I go off on the horse to muster a small holding paddock, during shearing.

'If the sheep are at the back of the paddock,' says the boss, 'bring them home along the fence. It will be slightly longer, but easier than bringing them over the hill. It'll be a breeze if you take A Dog.'

It is. I follow his instructions and arrive home with three sheep.

Shortly after, A Dog turns up with the remaining five hundred, having wilfully ignored me from the first sheep sighting, and brought them home over the hill.

'Take A Dog,' advises the boss when I tell him I can see that a small relation here on holiday is having trouble putting sheep through a gate on his own.

I duly take A Dog, up on the bike behind me, and speed to the scene. Almost at the gate, the bike splutters and dies, I dismount and between us, small helper on lethargic pony and me on foot, succeed in putting the sheep through the gate— without, of course, any help from A Dog. He is still sitting on the bike, gazing fixedly back to where he last saw the boss.

I wonder if things would change if I selected female pups instead of male.

GIVE HIM TIME

Angela Goode

Farmers are pretty pragmatic about their dogs. If they work, they'll live. And the honour of these most uncomplaining of jackeroos will be defended hotly.

The good dogs, the workers, are chauffered around all day in battle-scarred utes. They'll stand high on bales of hay, or smugly on the backs of a load of sheep.

A dog that won't work is useless. It doesn't matter that it's all happiness and joy, a wriggling, fawning body and darting, caressing tongue. A dog that doesn't work gets shot. Normally.

There is no point getting sentimental about them. No-one else wants them. One of the most impossible things to do in the country is give away a dog that won't work. But it is here that this tale of tough-minded practicality falters, for this is a story about one of those useless non-workers—a freeloader earmarked for an overdose of lead—who somehow survived.

Sam was a beguiling puppy, like most of them are. But what made him especially appealing was his breeding. His mother and father were out-and-out champions. They lived to work and did everything with pride and a sense of achievement. Sheep and cattle men queued to obtain pups of the duo, and those pups, through heat or sleet, went on to win widespread acclaim.

When Sam was born there was no question that he, too, would not follow in the footsteps of his hard-working clan. He was handed over to his new owner with the words: 'Give him time. He'll be a late developer. This line takes a while to mature.'

Prophetic words. Thirteen years later he still hadn't developed. In fact, in his whole easy-going life he did not do a day's work.

Oh, he liked riding in the back of the ute all right, and he was really expert at hanging on to the pillion seat of the motorbike as the boss mustered the cows. But ask him actually to get down among the action, to tail the mob down the road,

17

help in the yards, retrieve a breakaway, and he'd walk off, deaf to all protestations and pleadings. Insult him, and he'd sulk for days.

How Sam escaped going the way of other useless dogs, no-one quite knows. About a dozen times the rifle was loaded, but perhaps it was those words 'give him time' that kept coming back. The boss would again empty the chamber and put the gun back in the rack saying, 'He could come good yet. They said he was a late developer.'

But late developer or not, Sam was an embarrassment. No farmer worth his salt keeps a useless dog. If any visitors were around, Sam would be kept locked in his kennel . . . couldn't let anyone else see how he peeled himself away from the rest of the workers to sniff around rabbit holes, gaze at the corellas or snooze under the tea-trees.

Again and again, the boss tried to trigger Sam's instinct for work. Year after year, he tried. He begged, he cajoled, threatened and cursed. He was seen as a challenge to be conquered, a wayward to be tamed, a delinquent who just needed understanding. And so the old boy became a bit of a joke who had to see out his idle days in peace.

Once the jokes had started, it was too late. Who could kill a bloke who made us all laugh?

'He could come good yet,' the boss would say to gales of laughter about his grey-muzzled, arthritic old mate. 'It's not too late.'

Well, time did catch up with old Sam. Last week he died, his paws untarnished by toil and his record for laziness intact.

Perhaps it was all those champion genes that were to blame. Instead of workaholism, they produced a bloke with an analytical mind, a fellow who had too many brains for mere physical labour. He certainly had more fun than any other dog on the place. We've buried him down by the cattle yards, under his favourite tree—from where he used to watch all the other dogs earn their keep.

But you were lucky, Sam. We'll never be conned by the likes of you again.

PART 2

HUNTERS, LEADERS AND LONERS

A DIP IN THE DAM

Bruce Mills, Tumby Bay

Karla was given to me by a stud breeder friend in New South Wales and she arrived on the Indian Pacific train at Port Augusta.

My daughter and I picked her up: a pathetic-looking blue and tan pot-bellied kelpie pup, terribly smelly and covered in her own excrement. We washed her down under a tap near the platform. Her big eyes looked up at us all the while and the little tail wagged. After all that humans had put her through, she still called us friends.

Karla grew into a large kelpie, but was no world-beater in good looks—she had a blue-grey coarse-haired coat and one ear that never managed to stand erect—but as a clever worker, and in intelligence, she had few equals.

It seemed that whenever I left the station, my wife would get a call to say that there were sheep on the road, on the railway line, or somewhere else where they shouldn't be. Although we had at least six working dogs, Karla was always the one for that job. After showing her the rogue sheep, my wife would then drive the ute to the point where she wanted Karla to take them. Karla would then do the rest, no matter how difficult the task.

I remember one day when my brother was visiting and we went to a dam to check for stragglers. There were sheep near the dam so I sent Karla around them. Then I noticed some more sheep disappearing over a hill in the opposite direction. I said to my brother, 'Help Karla yard these sheep, while I go after the others.'

Not knowing the property, he noticed a gate into the dam enclosure and opened it. He tried to direct Karla and the sheep to it, but Karla completely disregarded his directions and took the sheep straight to the yards, penned them, and sat down in the gateway. My brother followed behind and on shutting the gate turned around to pat Karla, but she was on her way to help the boss—knowing I couldn't manage without her.

Another time, when the neighbour's yearling cattle were found on one of our dams, Karla again demonstrated her intelligence and persistence. Four cattle were on the dam and we had three kelpies with us.

The dogs were very excited as they hadn't seen cattle before. I sent them around the beasts and surprisingly they held them, first with eye, and then moved in aggressively with some nose bite. We decided to yard them in the sheepyards overnight.

Returning next day with the owners of the cattle and a large horse float and high portable gates, we intended loading the cattle there to save ourselves a long drive. Before we got organised, however, the yearlings jumped out of the yards. The dogs yarded three, but one went into the dam to escape the dogs. Karla immediately dived into the water and swam to the animal's head to try to turn it. The beast lunged up out of the water and came down on Karla. She came out coughing and sneezing.

I sent her straight back into the water and this time she swam up behind the beast and up its side to its ear which she barked into and bit. This turned the beast around. Then she dropped back and scratched at its tail with her swimming forelegs. Then she swam up the other side to redirect it, repeating the snapping at the ear and returning to the tail until she brought the animal into the shallows where we threw a rope over it and wrestled it into the horse float.

In hindsight, it would have been better to have driven the cattle home, but then we would never have witnessed the capabilities of this dog. Sadly, a few years later, we had to put this great canine friend down as she was suffering from cancer.

THE WONDER DOG

Mike Hayes

As I write, a chook is cackling like billyo over near the sheep yards, where a rude scar of freshly dug red earth mars the promising green of the new spring growth. It's Wal's grave, its site selected because, of all the places in the home paddock, it was there he'd have most liked to be—where he could doze in the sun, with the shearing plant buzzing soothingly in the background, safe in the knowledge that eventually he'd be whistled up to help put the mob back up the top paddock. I suspect that Wal wasn't really much chop as sheepdogs go. His achievements were rarely the sort of thing you'd boast about in the pub. But he was mine.

The news wasn't particularly heartening. Milly Duckwalk looked quite worried when she broke it to us. She was the wife of the new hobby farmer bloke with those huge flaming horses, the one who'd bought the fibro place on a couple of acres at the top end of the village.

'I thought I'd best tell you. Bill Potter just shot your pup's dad for killing lambs.'

Bill Potter's property was the largest of those immediately adjoining the village. Bill had seen the whole district change. The huge holdings, selected by pioneers like his ancestor, had gradually been split up into smaller blocks, most recently being snapped up by hobby farmers testing the water in their quest for a better lifestyle outside the urban dullness they were used to. With them came their naivety regarding the ways of the bush, their trendy ideas and their ratbag dogs.

Bill was a rare bird. He'd paid enough attention to the changes affecting the district to remain reasonably tolerant of the newcomers—both the two- and four-legged variety. Unlike others, more bitter, long-time local cockies, he was unlikely to go blasting away with his trusty twelve-gauge at a strange canine trespassing on his rolling acreage, unless there was a bloody good reason. And in the Duckwalks' case, it certainly wasn't merely a minor incursion by someone's footloose chihuahua, nipping through the Ringlock to gnaw on some tasty morsel of fresh cow-pat. No, the offender was Raglan, the Duckwalks' hulking great Alsation-Doberman-Pit Bull-Rotweiller cross. Apparently he'd been regularly raiding Potter's lambing paddocks, slaughtering the odd lamb or twenty, before carting the tastiest ones off to sample at his leisure.

'It didn't help that Raglan was actually eating one of the poor little things on the front doormat when Potter came around to see if we knew anything about his movements,' continued Milly dolefully.

Oh Dear! In fact—Double Oh Dear! You see, lying on our front verandah, gnawing diligently on an old gumboot in a manner probably not unlike dear-departed Raglan's lamb-chewing style, was a pot-bellied little black pup, about eight weeks old.

We'd called him Wally-Wally the Wonder Dog. Not only was he destined to be a partner in our burgeoning black wool empire, but he was also rumoured to be the son and heir of poor old Raglan. Not that anyone could actually prove it, mind you. Wally and about eight other slippery little devils had made a somewhat unwelcome appearance into the world at the nearby home of Claude Butcher, the village vet. Despite his vast knowledge of animal health, Butcher hadn't foreseen the lack of discrimination exhibited by Laverne, his promiscuous Kelpie-Collie cross bitch. When she came on heat, she'd attracted so many suitors, nobody could swear blind who'd sired the brood. It may well have been Wilfred, the postmistress's corgi, or even McHaughey, the big red setter from across the river, but Raglan's sheer size and determination to get his own way had to make him the main contender for the dirty deed. It didn't help the blame-layers that none of the pups resembled anyone but their Mum. That's often the way with sheepdogs, eh?

Whatever Wally's background, there was bugger-all we could do about it now. In the light of Milly's revelations, were we harbouring a monster? We couldn't really parcel him up and send him back to Claude, demanding our money back. The cunning bugger had let us have him free. In fact, he'd turned up at a barbecue at our place, with each of his own abundant offspring carrying a couple of wriggling, adorable puppies and, without even mentioning they were available for adoption, managed to get rid of the lot in the time it took him to eat a sausage sandwich and drink most of our beer.

The Child Bride, who was really the one who allowed herself to be conned into accepting Wal, hated herself in the morning. But by then, I too had been sucked in, realising that Wal could well be the live-in musterer we'd always wanted. In the past, we'd done our rounding-up by press-ganging crowds of useless humans (most of them softened up first by vast quantities of strong drink). We only had about twenty sheep in those days but, in order to get them to do anything, we usually had to do it on a one-to-one basis—one human musterer for each dusky ewe. Despite his questionable genes, little Wal represented some sort of light at the end of the mustering tunnel.

Wally had a pretty conventional upbringing, I suppose. There's nothing much you can do with a sheepdog pup until he's old enough to count to ten and recite the alphabet. Accordingly, his heritage was gradually revealed to him (but not the Raglan part).

He got to know sheep fairly early in the piece. We had, living temporarily in the backyard, two animals that more or less fit that description. Charlie Pride was an elderly, grotesquely fat Suffolk-Border Leicester cross with an appetite for anything that didn't move (and one or two things that did, especially young chicks and ducklings). Then there was Bunny, an equally grotesque black Border Leicester ram with an appetite for ewes of any age and bugger-all else.

Wal's major problem with Charlie was the latter's habit of breaking down any barriers to get at a decent feed of dog pellets. The adolescent pup was no match for the Galloping Gourmand and had to be fed indoors to avoid starving to death. Bunny the ram was a different problem again. At the back of what passed for his mind was a notion that the skinny, little black dog might indeed be a skinny black ewe. Wally wisely kept well out of his way—which didn't augur well for future confrontations in the paddock.

Wal's first encounter with the sheep as a mob augured even less well. He took one look at the ewes defiantly gathered in

24

a defensive circle in the village street—into which they'd found their unwelcome way after ripping the essentials out of yet another of our valuable antique fences—and fled home. But I persevered.

Training a working sheepdog isn't something you can learn from a book. If you go to the so-called experts, it's even harder. Some tie the trainee pup to a regular worker in the hope they'll stop struggling against each other and finally work out how to do the job together. It might work on Sesame Street, but from what I'd seen of the practice, all it taught the pup was how to gradually enjoy slow strangulation while totally stuffing up the technique of a perfectly good adult working dog (No letters, please!).

Most other theories tended to have a boarding school ring to them, involving beating, starving and abusing the students, and lots of cold showers. I took the gentler road—a combination of patience, practice and generally letting the dog do what he liked. The fact that it didn't always work is incidental.

Several times a week, we'd go together to a paddock at the fringe of the village and try to re-route our wethers through the fence joining us with the village common, hose them back up our paddock and tuck them neatly into what was once an old pigsty. Crikey, that was a long winter. Wal got the general hang of it all right, but he had an unfortunate habit of always putting the sheep between himself and the boss (me!). 'He won't git behind,' many a more-experienced dog handler kept reminding me. They weren't wrong, Narelle!

In desperation I decided to meet Wal halfway. I worked out a whole technique of mustering where Wal more or less did what he wanted to with the sheep while I compensated for his inability to 'Git behind.' As he moved the mob towards me, I'd back towards the yard. If we actually got them to the gate, we'd improvise as best we could. Those were heart-warming days of frustration and anger, and invariably ended up with the wethers splitting into individual escape parties and thundering back up to the farthest end of the common. However, Wal did manage to prove that if he couldn't quite handle a mob, he *could* pick out a single sheep and conquer it.

In later years this single talent proved invaluable when

25

selecting a killer out of the mob, isolating a fly-struck individual or taming some cranky ewe who'd hidden a lamb somewhere and had no intention of going anywhere with the rest of the flock. But that was later. The job immediately at hand was to get those wethers into the pigsty. We worked hard at it and eventually everything clicked.

On one particularly blustery, freezing, sleety winter's day, Wal actually dipped in behind the mob, held them while they decided whether or not to make a break for it and coaxed them into the tumbled-down shed at the far end of the sty . . . it didn't matter that they kept going through the ant-eaten slab wall of the rickety structure and completed their usual triumphant return to the common. We'd completed a muster. Wal and I had become a team. That's when I first experienced that warm inner glow which always followed a session with Wal.

Of all the many things I've tried in life, nothing's quite produced the satisfaction of working with a sheepdog. I once tried explaining it to the Child Bride, but she wouldn't have a bar of it.

'He smells and he barks all the time,' was all she'd say about that poor unwanted waif she'd naively accepted all those years ago.

Wal responded to her prejudice with total indifference. Above anything else, Wally was a one-man dog. I'm almost certain I was that one man. We'd both get the shits whenever an outsider joined us in the paddock. Even the best-meaning people have this funny, elitist attitude towards someone else's working dogs. They bellow nonsensical orders and when the poor old Holler Log quite rightly ignores them, he's written off as 'bloody useless.'

But it's always that useless dog that completes the task at hand. If Wal wasn't exactly Rin Tin Tin, it was hardly his fault. Despite any criticism that could be levelled at him by the pedantic and finicky, he lived up to his side of our partnership agreement as best he could. He was Boris Karloff to my Baron Frankenstein. So stuff 'em.

Nothing anyone could say could lessen that feeling of satisfaction, working with Wal. His successes were my successes. The failures? Well, any stupid bastard and his mongrel

26

could have pulled *them* off. Besides, many of the cockies who raised a quizzical eyebrow at Wal's little quirks were the sort of blokes who couldn't get anything done with less than a horde of 37 or so dogs, anyway. At least whatever Wal and I achieved—no matter how long it took—the success was due to just the two of us.

Thankfully, the spectre of his alleged father's homicidal tendencies being inherited never came to anything. In all our years together, Wal never bared a single fang at a single lamb. The nearest he came to it was when a sheep bit him. Charlie Pride, mistaking him for a giant black duckling, actually sank his shrivelled gums into Wal's haunch.

The only inkling we ever received that Wal's genetic soup might contain one or two little oddments that weren't normally found in sheepdogs came a couple of years later, when a local looney, Gumboots Farquhar, eyed him outside the post office and declared Wal 'the finest flamin' fighting dog I ever did see.' Gumboots was known to see quite a few things not normally discernible to the (sober) human eye, so at first I didn't pay a lot of attention. Then, out of the blue, he whistled up his own mutt, a hulking blue heeler called Fluffy, and ordered 'Sic him.' Poor old Wal, who was attempting to suck the last morsels out of a particularly inviting disembowelled possum in the middle of the road, looked up to find Fluffy descending upon him like an express train. He didn't have time to run and he didn't want to. Thinking Fluffy wanted a share of his gourmet's delight, he stood his ground. Seconds later, Fluffy was heading back up the road, mewing like a kitten. There was a side of Wal I hadn't seen before.

It happened again, years later, after Wal and I had helped a neighbour hose his rams back into their paddock. Wal was trotting happily back home when the neighbour's bull-terrier suddenly roared out of the back of his ute. The bull gripped Wal firmly by the throat. Apart from a yelp of surprise, Wal didn't bat an eyelid. He walked quietly over to a big red gum fence post and with the bull snarling and spitting but refusing to relinquish its hold, belted the savage little bastard a few hundred times against the sturdy strainer.

The surprised bull-terrier, possibly motivated by the very real fear of severe major fractures, suddenly gave in and fled. After that, other dogs tended to leave Wal alone. Bigger than the average sheepdog, he was more than able to take care of himself. But he never sought a fight and he never showed any savagery to sheep. It was more typical of him that, after the run-in with the bull-terrier, he hid in his kennel for three days, shaking like a leaf.

Oh, there were one or two little idiosyncracies I suspect neither Raglan nor My Good Self could really accept the blame for—one being Wal's habit of deciding he'd had enough and knocking off in the middle of intensely delicate negotiations with the mob. It usually occurred just when we'd almost succeeded in threading them through a particularly uncooperative gate. On such occasions, he'd slink off under the ute, where I had no chance of reaching him. There he'd lie, panting pathetically and regarding me balefully with his big yellow eyes, clearly telling me exactly where I could shove today's feeling of ecstatic satisfaction.

His worst habit was his uncontrollable urge to move his bowels over the interior of vehicles. God knows why he did it. When we were solvent enough to afford to register our old ute, it wasn't so bad, because Wal would get his rocks off (or out) all over the tray, but during the poor times, after the bloke at the local motor registry became hysterical with laughter at our request for a pink slip and we were forced to use the family car to travel between properties, Wal's defilement of the upholstery wasn't all that amusing. It happened without fail, usually along the stretch of road near the old lightning-shattered apple gum, exactly halfway between the home-spread at Tussock Flat and the outstation at Blacksnake. If we were really lucky, he'd also bring up the contents of his stomach not long afterwards. I knew how he felt.

The result of those indiscretions was the firm refusal by the rest of the family to join us on our excursions. Wal and I made the best of it by assuring ourselves that we didn't need anyone else on our team, anyway. Here we were, windows down in a feeble attempt to clear the air, hurtling through the silent bush, our ears (in my case, hair) streaming in the breeze . . . two footloose adventurers living life to the full. Our second property at that lonely spot called Blacksnake, on the Lachlan

River, became our personal domain. We'd share the thrill of the chase, the honest toil of the day's crutching and the happy brotherhood of the bush. We'd drive slowly home afterwards in a welter of comradeship, bone weariness, that indefinable feeling of satisfaction—and slowly drying dog shit. Then, out of the blue, it ended.

Wal had been fine when I fed him in the morning. He was still a bit shagged-out from the previous afternoon's mustering, but he slurped up his meaty bites with his usual gusto and settled down in the shade of his kennel. We came out later to do something or other with the chooks. The first inkling that something was wrong was the total lack of hysterical barking which usually heralded the presence of any of us around the yard. When I first noticed the silence, I imagined Wal had got off his chain. 'Bloody hell!'

In Wal's youth, every escape was a bit of a worry. We always feared the worst and that he'd loped off to terrorise a neighbour's flock, but in recent years, all Wal did was head straight for the defunct ute, now rotting quietly on flat tyres at the back of the machinery shed. He loved the battered old relic, remembering when it served as our valiant charger whenever we sallied forth to do battle with the woolly hordes at Blacksnake. It became his first port of call whenever he was freed from his chain. He was always optimistic about the possibility of it becoming suddenly resurrected to whisk us off for a day's satisfying yakka.

But this time Wal wasn't off the chain. This time there wasn't the slightest chance of a day's satisfying yakka. Wal lay in the shade of his doghouse, strangely still. He'd been dead an hour or so. There was no sign of what had stopped his noble heart. To all appearances, it had just given up the ghost like Wal did whenever he figured he'd done enough work out in the paddock. It had just knocked up in mid-muster. The silence became darker and deeper.

Like I said, we selected a possie at the head of the sheepyards to lay him down. It's still strange without him. Even the Child Bride admits it. Every time we hear a bark, we look up to see if it's Wal warning us of visitors, or an escape attempt by the goats, or another dog in the yard, or a bird flying overhead. Wal enjoyed issuing regular news bulletins and had a special,

29

identifiable bark for every eventuality. But, of course, these days it's not Wal at the newsdesk—just someone else's noisy bloody mutt bellowing for no apparent reason.

After the last winter's rains, the grass is growing back over the bare circle he'd inscribed around his kennel with his chain. His feed bowl's almost sunk into the ground. Even the cats have started taking for granted the fact that they can share his favourite sunny spot and loll contentedly on the warm iron roof of his old home. They've probably already forgotten about his indignant charges if they ever got too close to his food bowl. But I won't forget him. There'll always be a warm remnant of that deep satisfaction that only someone who's worked with a sheepdog enjoys.

The void left by Wal couldn't remain completely unfilled. A week before writing this, someone advertised for sale, in the local rag, a litter of sheepdog pups. God knows why I chose him, but I came home with a bleary-eyed little bundle, mostly white with a black smudge over one eye and that indefinable something that attracts a bloke to a dog. I suppose I could wax poetic about the streak of independence he showed compared to the other pups, or the way his ears cocked up when he noticed a mob of sheep in an adjoining paddock . . . but that'd only be wanking. I picked him because I liked him. That's a pretty good start to rekindling that magic I acquired from Wal. He will never be another Wal, but his name's Max and when he's old enough, he'll go out and carve his own niche in that mystic world only he and I can share.

GO, PLUTO!

Bill Sleep, Peterborough

Pluto came into my life as a foundling in 1972. One of the girls on the school bus which I drove at the time came to me and said, 'Would you like a puppy? I found him wandering on the railway line. I want to keep him but Mum says no. 'He's got big feet and will grow too big to keep in the town. Get rid of him.'

Mum proved to be right. He grew, not tall, but very strong and nuggetty; not savage, but aggressive, and he'd never knock back a fight no matter how tired. And he'd never give up until he came out on top.

He didn't receive any expert training but would always 'sit', 'come back', 'speak up' and so on when asked. The words 'Go, Pluto' would send him flat strap around the nearest mob of sheep, to bring them back to me equally as fast—and never mind any poor sheep that could not keep up. He'd get them next time and enjoy that just as much as the last trip. It was all in the game.

In August 1981 we were shearing, as we usually do at that time of the year. In the late afternoon, we had turned out about 400 ewe hoggets into our 1200-acre hills paddock as it was fairly cold with a south-west wind blowing. The hills had some shelter, being thick with low tussock bush and slate rocks standing out from the ground. There were also some gullies. However, around 8 pm the wind became a storm with intermittent showers and a threat of hail and possibly snow. Despite the shelter, the ewes were in danger of freezing and had to be brought to the shed.

I took Pluto and the ute and set off around the road to the north-east corner of the paddock and sure enough, there they were, just beginning to huddle up in the corner where there was no shelter—a recipe for disaster!

Abandoning the ute, Pluto and I set off to drive the ewes the two and a half kilometres back to the shed, straight into the gale, up over the hills. There were occasional showers and only starlight between the showers as the clouds raced by. There was no moon.

We got about halfway when two of the ewes started to knock up and needed my urging to keep them going while the rest strung out into the darkness ahead. After an exceptionally strong wind gust and shower, I suddenly realised that the mob had turned and disappeared back the way they had come and I was left with two sheep.

Knowing Pluto's habit of 'flat out and bring what comes' I was reluctant to send him back. However, I knew that if I left the two I had, they would die for sure. But then, if I did not get the rest, with the wind chill the way it was, they could all die. So it was 'Go, Pluto' and hope he brought at least some. The rest would have to take their chance.

I kept going with my two sheep for quite some time. Then, out of the darkness behind me, came the leaders of the mob, not flat out, but just trotting along with Pluto behind, working gently back and forth. Eventually we put them into the shed.

In another ute, we then went back to the far corner of the paddock for a quick look with the headlights. There were no sheep to be seen, so at about 1 am, I got to bed.

Next morning, with the weather clearer, we counted the sheep out of the shed. All were present. Pluto had brought them all!

ON HER OWN

Mary Noll, Wilmington

Years ago, my Dad had a farm at Murray Town and one also at Fullerville.

Dad owned a black kelpie dog, Jip, who at his command would take a mob of sheep to the Fullerville property completely unaided. The distance between farms was about four and a half miles. Dad would arrange for someone at Fullerville to open the gate. Jip would drive the sheep the distance, put them in the paddock and drive them to water. She would then wait at the open gate until Dad came and picked her up.

Jip did this job many times while Dad went on with other farm work.

At other times, Jip would take Dad's lunch in a basket, out to him in the paddock, along with any messages we wanted to give to him.

She was a much loved, beautiful dog.

THE GOAL SNEAK

M. Pearce, Arno Bay

Tiger was a dog with a terrific personality, and he left unforgettable memories of many humorous and outstanding incidents.

He was an Alsation-staghound cross, dark brindle in colour,

but with a generally gentle nature. He seemed to understand conversation which he interpreted quite quickly. For instance, if we were driving along the track in the old Chev, and the boys said, 'Let's give Tiger a race,' he would be off like a flash.

His main job was to kill kangaroos and foxes, but he also helped provide us with meat.

When we needed a rooster, we only had to show Tiger which one and he would follow it, then pounce on it and hold it, a paw on each wing until we arrived to collect it. Never did he harm the bird.

There was an old man kangaroo living on adjoining land which was mainly covered with scrub. He was so large and had injured so many dogs who had attacked him, that he had acquired the title of 'The Legend'. Due to his senior years, no doubt, he would fight rather than run.

The boys were riding their horses through the area and hoping they wouldn't meet The Legend because they weren't big enough or old enough to help the dogs if there was a confrontation. But sure enough, much to their dismay, there he was, large as ever, looking taller than seven feet and as wide across the rump as a Clydesdale horse. The boys decided to go quietly so as not to disturb him, but apparently his hearing was good.

When The Legend saw the dogs, he turned around and came towards them, intending as usual to demoralise the enemy. However, when Tiger, who had not previously been among the hunters, saw what was happening, he retreated a few yards to gain momentum, took a flying leap, and grabbed the offender by the throat. The weight and surprise of the attack overbalanced The Legend and gave Tiger supremacy.

After a struggle, Tiger was successful in killing The Legend.

Foxes in the area were always a menace. They killed poultry and lambs. Tiger, however, killed many foxes. Rabbits also had to be caught for feed for the dogs, and again Tiger was busy. As Tiger aged, he decided the easiest way to get them was to trot along the edge of the shelter scrub and snap them up in this jaws. The sheepdogs would chase the rabbits and Tiger would intercept them close to the scrub. Rarely did he ever miss. He was referred to as a goal sneak for his efforts.

SUGAR RAY HARRY

Milton Green, Bute

This happened in January 1985 when Dad and I, with our three dogs, decided to make our routine check of the sheep.

Our best dog is called Sugar Ray Harry and he is black. He got this name because of his unequalled fighting ability against the neighbour's dogs. We call him Harry for short.

The other two dogs with us were Cola, and Ricky, who was only young and learning the ropes.

We went around the sheep, which were in a fairly large paddock, and started heading home. We hadn't gone far when we noticed a fox which had been startled by the ute. It was running away hell for leather.

Since it was a big paddock, we thought we'd give him a run for his money. I stopped the dogs from jumping off while Dad tried to head him off and run him out of steam a bit. After a while, Harry got sick of this and decided it was time for action. So all three dogs jumped off and went after the fox.

The fox was fully grown and although he had run some distance, was still pulling away from the dogs. We headed him off a couple of times which tired him out a bit more, and also gave the dogs a chance to catch up.

Being cunning, the fox got through a fence and kept on running parallel to it. At this stage, Harry was about twenty yards behind, with the other dogs a bit further back again. We raced up past the fox with the fence between us, and the fox baulked and cut through the fence back into the same paddock.

By this time, the fox and the three dogs were getting pretty tired. Although they had caught up to him and had had a couple of snaps at him, he still led them by ten yards. The fox then ran into a dam with the dogs close behind. We were waiting for the fox to reappear out the other side, but he didn't.

We drove over to the dam and, to our amazement, there

was the fox swimming in the middle of the dam with the three dogs circling around the edge barking furiously. It was a small dam which contained in its centre about three feet of water. It was about twenty feet across.

Harry hated foxes. He'd seen what they did to young lambs. He jumped into the dam and swam to the fox, lunging at it to grab it by the throat. Due to the forces of gravity, both fox and dog sank to the bottom with the only sign above water being Harry's black tail waving vigorously. Seconds ticked by and then Harry rose to the surface, gasping for air. Not long after, the fox did the same. Harry again lunged at the fox and again both sank to the bottom.

This happened over and over again with the fox coming up considerably more slowly every time. Cola and Ricky, meanwhile, were circling the water's edge giving much needed vocal support while Dad and I rolled around the bank with laughter.

Eventually Harry, having conquered his foe, swam out to the bank and crawled out of the water for a victory shake. The fox eventually surfaced and also swam to the bank where what little life left in him was finished with the back of a shovel.

This is an incident I shall never forget. Harry's courage, fighting ability and determination were highly praised.

Now, Harry is eight years old and semi-retired. He has a dislocated shoulder and a bit of a prostate problem.

PART 3

WORTH ANY TWO MEN

And then there are the smart ones, the ones who know what to do without being told, who can count and find their way home, who know what's what and can do the job better than the boss!

THE ABATTOIRS DOG

Angela Goode

The local stock agent, Alan, lit up when we got talking about good dogs.

'In my forty years of working at saleyards, I reckon I've seen none better than old Whisky,' he said. 'He was the most intelligent dog I've ever worked with. I got him when I started work at fifteen and any task you set him, he would do.'

Alan and his brother Ross were drovers at the Gepps Cross saleyards on the outskirts of Adelaide. They needed good, strong, sensible dogs because the days often started before dawn and didn't end until after dark. They would spend each Tuesday unloading and yarding up animals in readiness for the next day's market. Then, after the sheep were sold, they had to move mobs to holding paddocks where they awaited slaughter, or straight to the abattoirs. Often, there would be mobs of lambs to walk to the irrigated pasture at the government sewage farm two and a half miles down a busy main road from the saleyards.

It was doing this job that Whisky made his name. Being newly-weaned and inexperienced at being mustered, lambs tend to scatter in all directions. To help keep them together, a bloke on a horse would go in front, and dogs and others on horseback would walk behind. These mobs would number between 1000 and 3000 lambs, and it took a bit of skill to get them over intersections without losing any.

Whisky accompanied Alan on one of these trips and, the following week, put himself at the front of the mob. No-one had instructed him. It was simply what Whisky chose to do. For six years, mobs of nervous lambs were led down Regency Road to the farm by this lone dog, and back again for slaughter, with never a one lost.

Alan says Whisky's style was relaxed and his manner casual. He used to lope along sniffing at posts, but if ever any lambs were going too quickly, he would authoritatively push them back into the mob. For some reason this shaggy black, white and tan kelpie cross was a born leader. If ever he had taken the wrong road, or lost concentration, there could have been sheep scattered far and wide.

An open drain carrying raw sewage ran through the farm and from time to time, lambs would fall in. Whisky had no fear of filth, so in he would dive, swim around the lambs and push them to the bank so someone could pull them out.

'It was lucky that Whisky didn't mind swimming in sewage, because none of us would have dived in after those lambs,' Alan says. Whisky learned the skills of a yard dog by being tied up near the end of the drafting race in the saleyards. From there, he watched the other dogs working. When he was let off in the afternoon of his first day there, he immediately threw himself into the job of drafting and penning up as professionally as any other dog in the yards.

Alan said he never needed any training, and seemed to know what any of Alan's commands meant—remembering that he had to pick, out of the noise and bustle, the words of his own particular master which competed with the whistles and calls of at least six other men to about fifteen dogs.

Every working day, Whisky would ride to the saleyards on the back of Alan's horse. The horse was nearly sixteen hands, but Whisky would leap onto its back and lie down just behind the saddle for the half-hour trot and canter to Gepps Cross from Woodville Gardens where Alan and Ross lived. On odd occasions, the horse lurched, causing Whisky to dig in his nails to keep his position. This would rather annoy the horse, which would buck. It must have been quite a sight, but the dog never fell off.

If ever Alan had to leave the dog at home for any reason on a Tuesday or Wednesday, there'd be hell to pay. Whisky would scream, bark and howl well into the morning—something he would never do on other days when he was left on the chain.

'Although there was absolutely no change to my routine, whatever the day, there is no doubt that he knew when it was sheep day,' said Alan. 'I am sure he knew the days of the week.'

COUNT TO TEN

Greg Twelftree, Minlaton

In the early 1960s we were given a puppy from a local farmer and named him Smith, after that farmer, Jim Smith.

The puppy turned out to be a very faithful, hard-working dog and this is a true incident.

We had yarded cross-bred lambs to send to market and our stock agent was helping us. We ran the lambs up the loading ramp into the truck. We realised six more lambs could be fitted in to complete the load.

My father called Smith and said, 'Smith, we need six more.'

With that, Smith ran down, cut six lambs from the mob and ran them up the ramp into the truck.

The stock agent, dumbfounded, asked, 'Good Lord, can that dog count?'

Dad replied, 'He's all right until he gets to ten. After that, he makes a hell of a mess of it!'

I'LL HAVE THIRTY-TWO

Wally Karger, Vale Park

A dog worth mentioning was a red kelpie owned by our neighbour on the River Murray. He wasn't a brilliant dog but useful in the yard. When dipping sheep after shearing, Toby excelled.

Jack, our neighbour, stipulated that twenty-eight sheep in the shower dip was the required number, but Toby always insisted on thirty-two.

How he knew we couldn't guess, but on counting the sheep out after dipping, we found he'd sent in thirty-two, no more, no less, every time.

No-one prompted him to send in that number, as he always ran over their backs, jumped down and drove them in by himself. Yet thirty-two was always the number.

EXACTLY EIGHT

Wally Karger, Vale Park

I sold some sheep to a chap at Kersbrook and he brought along a double-deck semi-trailer.

I offered Lassie to help load them, but he said his dog would do the job. And she did.

After he put eight sheep in the small pen against the cabin and closed the gate, his almost-white border collie bitch loaded the bottom and top pens on her own with exactly eight sheep in every one.

A TOTAL WORKAHOLIC

Max Verco, Marcollat

Every now and again you get an outstanding dog, a champion. Well, Joker was one of those.

In the 1930s, I worked on a property in the Flinders Ranges. Central Mount Stuart was on this place. The country was very steep and the ranges were terribly craggy. The scenery was magnificent, but, oh, it was very hard country to work. You were constantly up and down rocky mountains, with lovely native pines on their slopes and creeks at their base.

Joker lived with me out on camp. It was only him and me. We became very close. He used to come inside the building but it was a pretty rough old place and only had dirt floors. There were no beds in it, so I cut some pine logs and nailed a few bags between them to save me camping on the floor. It was a little bit of luxury. In the really cold weather, old Joker used to sleep on my feet.

Now, when I was mustering in those ranges, I used to ride along on the top of the range. The idea was that I would chase the sheep off the top of the range down the steep slopes to the valleys on either side where it was easier travelling for the sheep and horses. About half way down one side of the craggy range, I'd place a man and his horse, and another horseman down at the base. The bloke half way down would pick up my sheep and push them down to the next bloke, who would collect them and drive them along the creekbeds to the end of the range. On the other side, I needed only Joker to do the work of these two men on their horses. I only had to show him the job once, and ever after that he knew that he was the bottom man. He had so many more brains than any other dog. If there were sheep halfway down, he would go up and get them and take them along. When we got to the end of the range, he'd have his mob, and the other two fellows would have theirs.

When I left there, I got a job on a station in New South

Wales. I went round by boat from Adelaide, and when I went in to get my ticket round to Sydney, I told the people in the office that I had a very good sheepdog and that I wanted to take him with me on the boat. They told me to put him in the care of the butcher. I told them I was very fond of this dog, that he was a mighty dog, and to tell the butcher to really look after him, or we would have an argument at the end of the trip. By that he had to make sure the dog had food, water, a bed, and didn't fall overboard, or I would deal with him.

It only took three or four days to get around to Sydney. When I went to get old Joker from the butcher, he was like a bloated toad! This butcher, he looked after him all right. I reckon he used to sling him a shoulder two or three times a day. Old Joker could hardly walk. It was a hell of a shock for a dog used to getting only a few scraps out of my saddlebag when we were out for a week at a time in that tough country.

When I got up to the station, because he was so good, I was straight away dropped in to all the best droving jobs. If I hadn't had a top dog, I would have got jobs like cleaning out the sheep manure from under the shearing shed, doing a bit of fencing, all the odd jobs. It's much more fun out droving with your horse and dog.

Joker and I did a lot of droving. Once, in 1932, I was bringing a mob down from New South Wales to Hallett in South Australia. We were out on the road for about six weeks. Out in that back country, there were no fences. You just let the mob spread. I was the youngest on the team, so while the others had a feed, I got the job of riding slowly around the mob to keep them more or less together. I only had to do that for two or three days, and then I just gave old Joker a sign.

Every dinner time after that, he'd take over. I'd go into the camp with the men while we boiled our billy and had a bit of tucker. Joker would start one side and gradually work his way right around the mob, just easing a few in here or there that were heading out. Pretty well every day, it would take him almost twenty minutes to do the round. We used to time him! When he got opposite us he would look over at me and I'd just wave again, and he would start on his way back.

43

There wouldn't be many dogs you could teach to do this. Most would go around them if you sent them, but they'd push the sheep in on you, and have them milling all around the camp. Joker loved his job and was never happy unless he was working. He was a total workaholic.

Dogs are pampered today. My dog now rides on my motorbike, but in those days, they had to trot by your horse for two or three hours before you got out into the paddock. They were tough dogs.

In those days there was no refrigeration, and in that country, it was as hot as hell. We had to salt all our meat, and when you were out on camp, you had salt meat and damper and hot plum jam. You didn't eat much. You couldn't. It was hot. You'd toss a bit to the old dog, and that's about all he had— a bit of old salt meat.

He couldn't stop working. When we got some chooks, he didn't know what they were but being a good sheepdog he loved to round them up just because they moved. I used to scold him a bit. I'd say, 'Hey, you shouldn't be rounding up chooks'—and look, he knew. I'd creep along the side of the shed and he'd look around and see me looking, so off he'd go, as though he had no interest in a chook at all. He'd cock his leg on a tree or something and wander away as though it was the last thing on his mind. He was nearly human.

THE RABBIT TRAP

Errol Crossing, Berri

I had a grazing property at Tungkillo where I taught Towser to catch fly-blown sheep for me.

Being rough and stony country, I used to ride on horseback around my sheep. Towser would sniff out the blown sheep so I could treat them in the paddock.

I was doing this one day when Towser took off after a sheep. I called him back, knowing it wasn't fly-blown, as they had just been shorn.

He ignored my whistle and calling, knocked the sheep over and held it. I rode up to chastise him for not doing as he was told.

That sheep had a rabbit trap on its foot. He knew it had to be caught.

Towser lived to be eighteen years old.

HE FOUND HIS OWN MOB

Bruce Mills, Tumby Bay

Spike was quite a character. He had one glazed eye, obtained after a kick from a horse which he loved to tease. A good, hardy worker, he was always ready to go, and he was a great mate for a young fellow (as I was in those days.)

It was mustering time, and we were in thick mallee country,

45

west of the Middleback Range. My mate and I set out from the homestead, on the east side of the range. We were on horseback and accompanied by Spike. Our destination was an old caravan which had been placed by a mustering paddock and dam a few days earlier. It had been equipped for a week's mustering.

About three and a half miles from our destination, we saw a mob of sheep camped on the edge of a clearing, with very thick scrub behind them. The sheep saw us and stood up. Knowing that the scrub was very thick and hard to gallop through, we decided to send Spike around the sheep.

Now Spike, in spite of his faults, had a very good cast. Away he went, and we waited for ages for him to move the sheep, but nothing happened. The sheep started to drift off into the scrub. We decided that Spike must have put up a kangaroo (his main fault!) and left the sheep. After much scrub bashing and many scratches we turned the sheep ourselves and, cursing the useless dog, we took them to camp.

We arrived there at sundown, and, after seeing to the horses' needs, set to getting something to eat for ourselves.

I was worried about my dog. I thought he must have been ripped open by an old scrubber kangaroo and was probably lying injured or dead out in the scrub somewhere. We were just about to climb into bed when we heard movements in the bushes outside. On investigating, we found the caravan ringed with sheep, held there by Spike.

No doubt in his original cast, he had found another mob of sheep further out and had followed us into camp with his own mob.

Spike had never been to this camp before and to get there had had to find and negotiate a narrow neck in the salt lake, a fact we checked out next morning. Needless to say Spike received much praise and a good feed, and I slept well.

BACK IN TOWN

Stella Tiller, Balaklava

We live in a small country town, in semi-retirement, so our tan kelpie, Toby, was kept on the farm where our son and his family live.

However, Toby went everywhere with my husband in his ute. The farm is about two miles as the crow flies, or about three by road, from our home.

At one stage, my husband had to go away for about three weeks. He took his ute and left Toby at the farm. He arrived back late one night and put the ute in the shed at the house in town. He left the shed door open.

Next morning, Toby was in the back of the ute waiting to go to work. He hadn't been to our place in town during those three weeks.

How did he know the ute was back? Could he smell it, or my husband, or both from that distance?

CHAUVINISM ON THE FARM

Muriel Freeman, Port Neill

Most farmers' wives will be able to relate to this incident which occurred about twenty-seven years ago. I still get a laugh when I think of it.

We had just taken over our farm which had very rundown fences and sheepyards. It had no gates and sheep-handling was very difficult.

The workforce was one husband with a very short straw as far as temper goes, one very young, untrained sheepdog, and me, a virtual newcomer to farming. We coped reasonably well, bringing the sheep home from the very farthest paddock, two miles, with one husband and one dog sitting in the ute and me droving the sheep along by foot. The dog was relegated to my seat after the first 100 yards as he was too fast, ran through the middle of the sheep, and had sheep lying down and scattering in all directions.

He was a very smart dog.

On arriving at the yards and after many words of wisdom on how to yard the sheep, we eventually had them in the drafting and 'holding' yards. As there were no gates, the dog and I had to keep pushing the whole mob of 2000 up from behind, while keeping them away from the outer fences. We had reduced the mob down to a manageable number so I asked the boss if we could stop for a drink break.

'No,' he said, 'not until we finish.'

It was a long, hot, hard day's work. He had me at it from 8.30 am until three in the afternoon. The dog, however, was quite fresh.

A HERITAGE
OF COUNTRY GENES

Angela Goode

When I left the city to marry the boss and live on a sheep and cattle station, one link with my city days did remain. That was my faithful and much loved Lucy. Originally a pup from an abandoned dogs' home, she was a border collie who for eleven years subjugated her rural instincts to live amongst asphalt and cement.

We had always spent a lot of time in the bush, when at weekends I would saddle up my horse and ride through the back tracks of the Adelaide Hills. She would follow me for hours, checking out the smells and delights on the way.

During the week, she would be the ultimate city girl, bringing my morning paper to me, guarding the house during my absences at work, and going for runs before or after work with me. I would ride my bike and she would gallop along the footpath.

Actually, when I said that she would guard the house during the day, that's what I thought she was doing. It was only after some years that I discovered that as soon as I had left for work, she would thump open the gate, squeeze through and head for the shopping centre. There she would camp all day on the footpath outside the butcher shop and next to a bakery, being fed slices of sausage, buns and pies by the people who got to know her. (I had noticed that she had put on weight and had accused my elderly neighbour of throwing his scraps over the fence.) She would always be home waiting for me when I finished work.

I had always felt a bit guilty about having a sheepdog living in the city, even though I was giving her plenty of exercise. I felt bad about making her live in a place that clashed with her heritage of rural genes and away from the working life for which such dogs are bred.

After tiring of her shopping expeditions, Lucy tried another tack to make life in the city less boring. I was working at a radio station in the University of Adelaide and would ride my bicycle into the city each day. Lucy took it upon herself to find out where I went. She had never seen where I worked.

I was in a meeting about an hour after arriving one day when someone came in and said a very excited black and white dog was scratching at the front door. He opened the door and straight into the meeting room galloped my overjoyed companion. I felt a whole series of emotions at the same time— pride at her ability, anger at the danger of crossing city streets, shame that she was so lonely, delight that she was so devoted. She could only have followed the scent of my bicycle tracks on a route that took her through the heart of the city and six sets of traffic lights.

Once the game had started, I had no hope of keeping her at home. I chained her up, but she arrived with the clip hanging from her collar. I got a new chain and she arrived without the collar. I got a new collar and she arrived dragging a section of chain. I tied her to the tank-stand and fully expected her to come dragging the tank.

A vote among staff members determined that she could go on the payroll as recreation officer, so until I left to travel to Western Australia she accompanied me every day legitimately, running along footpaths while I cycled.

In Western Australia, we stayed on my brother's farm and that was her first introduction to sheep. It was as if all those generations of working dog genes exploded at once. Her face lit up, her body tensed with excitement and, given the opportunity, she would work in paddock and yards until her sides were heaving. I left her with my brother when I journeyed north and he was most reluctant to part with her when I returned.

I went to Melbourne for university studies and Lucy went too. However, I was away from my house from early in the morning until late at night and she again found life too boring. She decided to register a complaint by wrecking the garden, chewing through the back door, destroying the screen on a window and munching through the curtains. I got the message and sent her back to Adelaide by train the next day. She grinned all the way down the platform, wheeled on a trolley in one of those wooden cages with iron bars.

I would drive home to Adelaide about once every three months and my parents said that every time, well before I reached their house, she would leap up, all alert and delighted, and bound to the front gate. When I pulled up in my old car, she would always be there wagging and squealing with joy. She had somehow memorised the pitch and thump of the engine. No other vehicle produced this reaction. She was never there on the day I left to return to Melbourne, always disappearing to avoid the farewell.

Actually, several times I nearly had to say farewell permanently to her. Once, when she had severe gastroenteritis, she decided to end it all. She dragged herself outside and lay in the blazing sun on a piece of corrugated iron. A good vet pulled her through but she had not been far from death by the time I found her.

Another time, she fell into a ground-level open water tank. She must have been swimming around for over an hour trying to get out. Her front paws were bloody stumps where she had desperately scratched at the walls. She was barely keeping herself afloat. Her eyes and nostrils were all that were out of the water. When I dragged her out, she lay, heaving—a sodden, half-drowned wreck—until she recovered enough to lick her gratitude.

When we went to live in the bush permanently, Lucy was in her element. She could do a bit of sheep work, although her enthusiasm was sometimes more than the boss could cope with.

She abandoned the domestic scene for entire days spent in the back of the ute doing important things like tagging calves, fixing gates and pulling windmills. My tasks couldn't compete with that lot and I did feel a bit rejected. But to see that dog shining with health and loving her new life was some compensation. She lost the middle-aged spread acquired from soft, city living.

When the boss wasn't winning her over with his glamorous jobs, Lucy and I would go for long walks. It was with her that I explored my new domain. Together we waded through the creek and together we hunted through sheds and pushed through the scrub. Her enthusiasm for life on the land was infectious. Although I had spent holidays in the bush before, and loved it, it was her boundless joy for each new day and its tasks that helped me assimilate into the ranks of seasoned country women.

As time went on, Lucy grew blind and deaf. She would track me around the farm by following the scent of my footsteps. Her hips were a bit rickety and she spent long hours sleeping in her basket.

One day, just as she used to disappear to avoid farewells when I returned to Melbourne, she walked off into the bush. She was seventeen and ready to die. We found her body after a few days and buried her at the bottom of the garden. We planted a West Australian flowering gum over her.

She was my last tangible tie with the city, the last visible remnant of my former life in the world beyond dirt roads and rolling paddocks.

She, with her heritage of country genes, helped me become one with the land.

ON AUTOMATIC

Bill Franklin, Cowell

Our border collie, Bob, was a great sheepdog, but this incident concerns the house cow.

Every day, Bob would go and fetch the cow for milking, whenever he heard the rattle of the milk bucket.

By the time one of us had walked from the house to the milking shed 300 metres away, Bob would have the cow waiting in the yard.

One morning, however, some months after we had sold the house cow, I had reason to use the old milk bucket.

I was amazed when, about half an hour later, Bob turned up with the Jersey from the adjoining farm two kilometres away.

SIX MONTHS ACROSS THE GULF

Dick Mills, Kanmantoo

A few years prior to the First World War my grandfather, WG Mills, MHR, assisted his second son, Richard, to purchase a property near Elbow Hill, south of Cowell.

It fell to Alec, my father, to take across a flock of sheep from Millbrae to Cowell to stock the place. Alec was seventeen or eighteen years old at the time.

The sheep were driven by him on foot to Port Adelaide, then loaded aboard a lighter. The dog, called Shep, was of great assistance to Alec and travelled with him and the sheep to Cowell. Here the sheep were unloaded and Shep assisted to get them to the farm down along the coast.

One can just imagine the fond pat that Shep got when finally the paddock gate was shut. That pat was even fonder than Shep imagined it would be because he was to be left behind to assist Richard on the farm. After a few days' stay to acquaint himself with the country his brother had taken up, Alec returned by the next regular ship to Port Adelaide. He then travelled back to Millbrae at Kanmantoo.

Soon after Alec left the new farm, Shep disappeared. Alec

knew nothing of this until eventually the news reached him via letter. Alec resigned himself to the loss of another good dog. This was not an uncommon occurrence and new dogs were constantly being bred and trained.

Time passed by after the letter. Winter came with green grass coming in the paddocks again, and the cry of new-born lambs was heard across the valley. Lamb-tailing passed, then shearing.

Then, one bright morning, Alec opened the back door and there was Shep, wagging his tail with great joy. There was a very fond reunion and the family at Millbrae was amazed to think that a dog could find its way across the gulf.

It had taken him six months to complete the journey.

SIXTY MILES HOME

Clare Lawrie, Naracoorte

During the war years, most of us had to be useful, either indoors or out-of-doors.

To help my brother at Waikerie, in the Riverland, with the mustering for shearing, I travelled with my sheepdog, Kim, by train from Copeville in the Murray Mallee

We had quite a few successful days getting the sheep together.

One evening, I forgot to tie Kim up. The next morning, he had gone. I rode all over the district trying to find him, with no luck.

Shearing ended and I went to Adelaide to meet my husband who was coming down on leave from the Darwin area.

A fortnight later, I had a phone call from my father at Copeville telling me that Kim had found his way home. He was very footsore and weary. Naturally, I was more than delighted to get the news. I have often wondered, though, how he did it. Copeville was over sixty miles from Waikerie.

Since Kim had travelled there in a dog box, he wouldn't have seen where he was going.

I'M SURE IT WOULD BE HELPFUL ...

David and Nancy Pearce, Maitland

King didn't need any training, nor did he have fancy casts. He could work out where the sheep had to go and so got on with the job. He seemed to like to have a human with him, but just for companionship.

We are crop farmers as well as graziers, so it was customary for King to travel out to paddocks being ploughed, reaped or whatever. He would go a couple of rounds behind the implements, checking all was well. Then he would rest at a suitable corner of the paddock until lunch, when he would expect a ride home.

One day, we were working in a paddock that had a few acres of scrub. About 400 ewes and lambs were grazing there. For some reason, King got left behind when we went home for lunch.

Perhaps that's what set his mind to tick over like this: 'My man usually invites me to ride home with him, but not today. I wonder if he's intending to draft those lambs off. He did mention it. I'm sure it would be helpful if I took the sheep home, while he's having lunch with his wife.

'He's even left the gate open, too. He doesn't usually do that unless he is moving sheep.'

So off he went and delivered, right to the back gate, the ewes and their lambs, who are often difficult to keep in one mob.

The amazing thing was that he did the job in less than an hour. It took us one and a half hours to return them to the paddock—with the help of two humans.

We still wonder how he managed to get the lambs and ewes past all the trees without losing any. Then he took them over the crossroads at the paddock gate where the mob could have gone in any of four directions. The last leg of the trip was along the busy main road, before he was able to turn up the driveway.

WE'RE MATES FOREVER

DA Treloar, Wiawera Station, Olary

I don't have a story as such, but I have a poem. I wrote it in the middle of our last drought while I was sitting in the truck waiting for the pump to fill my water tank. I was carting water for the house, for showers and toilet only. It was roughly a 14-mile round trip. All but one of our dams were dry and the wells and bores were forking and breaking down all the time.

I have been looking after the place for Dad, most of the time on my own, for the past two and a half years as he had to go to Yaramba Station when my brother left. So I was really flat out and felt at the end of my tether and didn't know where to turn. I had lost the use of over 45 square miles of our 90 square mile block due to bores and dams packing up on me.

My dogs, Red and Jed, were the only comfort I had. That is why I wrote this poem. It is actually what happened. I had been trying for months to get the squatters tank full, or even a foot in it, to no avail as the well kept forking.

One hot night I went over to check it only to see a trickle flowing in. I lay down on the top and thought, 'Oh, shit, what am I going to do?' I felt really lost. Then my two dogs Red and Jed ran up the side of the tank pillar and started to whine and lick me. They knew I was upset and I'm sure they were trying to cheer me up. They did. It got me going again, and it rained within another month.

They're both good working dogs and I love them both.

Now that I've explained the situation a bloke was in, maybe you'll understand what I meant to say in the poem.

There is no doubt that if you have a good dog and treat him kindly, he will understand your condition or feelings and worry about you when you're not so good. They're the best mates you can get, I reckon.

RED DOG

I sat there on the old stone tank,
Watching the salt water trickle in,
Worrying about the money we haven't got in the bin,
And this bloody drought,
That we could do without.
Listening to the old pump jack grinding away,
In its slow methodical way,
Whilst catching the blood red sunset of another stinking hot
    day.

Gazing occasionally to the west and east,
Hoping for one cloud at least.
There was not one in sight,
And the bloody wind refused to blow,
So the windmills stayed still,
And the stock tanks wouldn't fill.
The sheep were hanging around,
Waiting for that liquid gold to come out of the ground.
They were all dying for a drink,
And reckoned their lives were on the brink,
'Cause the troughs were as dry as the empty kitchen sink.

The bores were breaking down and the dams were nearly dry.
It was enough to make a grown man cry.
Then up on to the tank jumped my old mate Red,
Close by my little black kelpie Jed.
They both gave me a slobbery lick,
As if to say shit a brick.
We're mates forever,
So pick yourself up and we'll stick this drought out together.
So I sat up straight instead of half on my back,
Figuring they've got the right idea Jack!
And thinking as it got further into the night,
I'm not going to give in without a bloody fight.
Hoping all the time the good Lord up above would hear my
    cries,
Before everything withers up and dies.

A PARTICULARLY GOOD 'EYE'

Margaret Hancock, Bute

Toby was the greatest sheepdog this farm has ever seen. A black and white animal, Toby is remembered as a well-trained dog with a heap of natural ability and a particularly good 'eye'. He must have been some dog. At shearing time, his exploits are told and retold every year, especially if there is someone new in the shed.

During shearing the order to 'Go fetch the woolly ones' would send him off past the newly-shorns to the back paddock where the self-satisfied woollies grazed unsuspectingly. A quick skirt around the fence to check for strays and he would soon have the mob in a nice little bunch, edging them through the gate and up to the yards.

He was as reliable as the sunrise and worth any two working men. Like all farm dogs, he was a constant companion to his master, no matter what the job. It was on one of these non-sheep jobs that Toby became almost immortal—well, his memory did anyway.

The men were fencing and Toby watched everything intently. He scratched the dirt as he pretended to dig post holes, and he supervised the wire-straining strand by strand. He walked twice as many miles as the men—backwards and forwards. He chased birds and had some fun with a hare.

By sundown, Toby had had a full and satisfying day. The men packed their gear into the dray and rode home. Nobody noticed that Toby was missing until someone went to feed him. There was a scramble as the lanterns were lit and a couple of fellows went back to the day's work site. Was Toby hurt? Had he been run over by the dray? Perhaps he had got upwind of a neighbour's bitch.

Nothing so mundane would have caused Toby's story to be recalled so often

When the men arrived back at the day's task, there was Toby—lying midway between two fence posts staring at the fence. The lanterns revealed the men had got the wires crossed.

Folk who recall this event insist that this was not a shaggy dog story.

PART 4

TIME OUT

We all need to stop work sometimes, whether it's to vote in town, go to a dog trial, or just because it's tucker-time. It seems some of us, though, take a break for no reason at all.

THE VERY LAST LAP

DH Turnbull, Cleve

As a young man, I spent many long hours driving a horse team to clear a scrub block.

My black and white border collie, Spotty, would come out in the morning behind the team and follow for the first round of the paddock. He would then spend the rest of the day sitting around the lunch box or sniffing out rabbits.

Then, with some uncanny sense of timing, he would follow the team for the very last lap of the paddock before knock-off time.

Only once did he make a mistake and have to do two laps.

THE YARD DOG FUNDRAISER

Angela Goode

We thought we'd run a yard dog competition at the local school fete. It was a good way, we reckoned, of getting the men along to what was traditionally a pretty tedious affair.

So the research was done and the experts gathered and showed us what to do. We set the course up in a paddock adjoining the school, alongside the side road. In one corner, we put a yard for all the sheep that would, in groups of ten, be pushed by the competing dogs to another yard. In this yard, there was a drafting race and a ramp leading to a truck. The dogs would have to help draft the sheep and then push a few up the ramp and then unload them again.

Nothing like this had been held in the district before, so interest in the event was running pretty high. Every bloke, of course, thinks his dog is the best; but all the pub talk and bragging in the world won't necessarily convince anyone else that this is so.

The idea of doing the sort of work that's done on the farm to test out the dogs in public made sense. On the day, eighteen, dogs and owners turned up to compete for the $100 prize. Winning was pretty important, so tension was high. There were a few brawls between ragged-eared mutts around the wheels of the utes, a fair bit of yelling by their owners and a huge crowd of spectators around the fences.

Most of the dogs, though, were experienced workers who had been around yards and sheds for years. They weren't much bothered by the people and noise. They loped around on the end of their chains, taking the scene in calmly through narrowed eyes, and marking out their territory on evey ute wheel and fence post.

The young dogs, the ones that their bosses had high hopes for, were in a frenzy of delight. They were beside themselves with joy that all these people and children with ice-creams had gathered to entertain them. They would drag their red-faced owners from one child to another, getting pats and giving licks, and ignoring all calls for reason.

When the competition finally got underway, the dogs and owners assembled up one end of the ground, near the top yard. The judge stood in a tyre on the ground in the middle of the paddock so he could observe every movement of the competing dogs. Timekeepers and other officials went to their allocated spots.

The whistle blew and out came old Bluey. This efficient old dog only had eyes for his sheep and ears for his master. With head down and rump in the air, he coerced his jumpy wethers down through the race and dispatched them through the gates in a display that was slick, quick and looked boringly simple. What followed made Bluey's effort seem even more masterful. Out came Susie. She hadn't had a lot of experience, and she was terribly excited about being there at all.

She wriggled and squirmed at the end of her lead. She rolled and jumped on her boss's legs. The whistle blew. The sheep were let out and Susie's lead was unclipped. With great speed, she flew at the sheep and barked wildly. They scattered like sparks off a wheel, and then ran in blind terror.

Now the fence alongside the paddock was pretty good as far as some farm fences go. It wasn't made, however, to cope with the force of a mob of heavy sheep galloping full tilt. Susie, ignoring her furious master's commands, was having a great time. Her sheep hit the fence. Its slack wires parted and Susie's mob galloped to freedom down the road and towards the shopping centre.

This unanticipated entertainment was greatly enjoyed by the onlookers, some of whom raced down the road after the sheep. Susie was eliminated and her owner, trying to laugh off the humiliation, took himself to the bar.

The next contestant, a cool-headed brown kelpie, looked as though he'd be a bit dull after the sprightly Susie. He was giving a faultless display, but suddenly he lost concentration. His owner whistled, and whistled again. The kelpie—Mick was his name—put his nose on the ground and started following some scented trail through the grass.

Now the rules for the competition stated that no bad language could be used. Owners could help their dogs control the sheep, could speak and whistle as much as they liked, but they were not allowed to swear or lose their tempers. Mick's owner, a popular bloke who had been laying bets that Mick would finish in the first three places, was having a hell of a battle. He shouted, he roared, he hit the side of his leg with a stick—but Mick was entranced. The mirth of the crowd around the barriers made the poor man even more red-faced and furious.

Mick found the source of the aroma. It was a chop from the barbecue that someone had dropped. Mick grabbed it and lay down in the grass with it between his paws to deal with it. Striding up behind him, Mick's boss shoved the dog with his boot. But Mick wouldn't be moved. He finished his chop, got up, had a pee against a post, and then trotted back to the sheep to finish his test. The owner was furious and even more so when rumours circulated the ground that the chop had been put there by one of his rivals.

63

One by one, the dogs tackled the course. When another mob of sheep was driven through the fence—but this time, the fence leading into the schoolyard—the organisers realised there were easier ways to raise money. Having ten crazed wethers dashing through sweet and cake stalls, frightening the ponies giving rides, and hurtling through the plant stall doesn't do a lot for the reputations of the local dogs.

The day did end with three proficient, sensible dogs scoring the ribbons—but the dogs everyone remembered were the idiots, the enthusiasts and the disobedient.

The following year, no-one felt like staging another competition. We had a dunking pool instead.

THE TRAVELLING MUSICIAN

Fay Story, Tumby Bay

After a year working sheep at the farm where my son Tim worked, Bomber came to live with us. Tim had got a job in a town.

He was a black and white dog which Dad often threatened to shoot because he was always found sitting in the car's driver-seat. This habit of his was perhaps our first indication of Bomber's love of travel.

Not having sheep on our small farm, Bomber became a pig dog who was expert at finding the boar in each paddock of dry sows.

In the last term of our youngest son Keith's school life, Bomber started school. This began one day when the school bus was travelling homewards. The bus was rounding a corner when Keith saw him and asked the driver if he could pick him up.

Quite often after that, Bomber would be found waiting at the door of the bus when the final siren rang. He would walk into town just so he could get a bus ride home. The other pupils on the school bus loved Bomber and he loved the attention.

The feat of actually finding the right bus was in itself remarkable as there were five which delivered pupils in many different directions from Tumby Bay. On only one day did he make a mistake. A teacher found him sitting in the wrong bus and told Keith.

One day, Keith left school early to play the Last Post at a funeral. We arrived home just prior to the arrival of the school bus at the gate. Instead of going straight past, it drew to a halt. The door opened and out hopped Bomber. He turned around, wagged his tail to say 'thank you' to the driver and trotted home. He looked at us as if to say, 'Well, here I am. Where were you?'

Living only a few kilometres from the sea, we often go swimming. Bomber also loves the sea and on hot days sometimes goes off on his own, returning home in the evening tired and salt-encrusted.

One afternoon, our son was out in the boat fishing off a reef. He spotted a black head swimming towards him. It was Bomber, who was duly heaved over the side to spend the rest of the day in the boat.

When my husband worked at the local hardware store, Bomber would often arrive at the farm utility just prior to lunch, having had a swim, and being ready for a ride home.

You will be thinking that this dog should have been tied up more often. He often was, but if he looked as if he was in the mood to sleep on the mat at the back door, I would weaken and let him off the chain. When I turned my back, he would be gone.

Many times, I've driven into town and gone straight to the jetty to find Bomber. He would have had his swim, and at my call, he would bound into the vehicle and smile at me as if to say, 'Thanks for getting me.'

But while Bomber was something of a traveller, he was certainly no musician. We have a family of five and all are musical so we formed an old style dance band. During practice sessions at home, when the trumpet hit a certain key, Bomber would lift his head and howl, doing his best to accompany the player. He certainly was not in tune, though.

One quiet evening, when I was attempting to tape the Last Post for an RSL dinner, my son would get to a certain place in the music and Bomber would join in. This came out quite clearly on the tape. We eventually recorded the piece inside and Bomber was not on the final tape.

TUCKER-TIME

Mrs AM Turnbull, Cleve

Biddy was my father's dog, a border collie.

One day, when my father was riding near the boundary fence, he saw two sheep just inside the neighbour's paddock. One was ours and one the neighbour's. My father sent Biddy around these sheep, but they disappeared up the gully and out of sight over the ridge.

After a considerable length of time, Biddy returned. She had one sheep with her. It was the one with our brand.

Another day, this clever dog was in the laundry and she was trying to attract our attention. She was jumping up at the butcher's knives and killing-gear hanging up in there.

When my father followed her outside, she had all the ration sheep yarded.

She must have thought it was time to have some fresh meat.

THE THIEF

Stuart Clements, Kimba

Our large, yellow dog called Tiger has one fault. He is a thief.

We keep meat in the workshop in a fridge, but the plastic bags of meat started disappearing. I blamed my wife for giving too much meat to the dogs, and she blamed me.

One morning, however, the workshop door was left open and we became suspicious. We decided to keep watch, and, before long, Tiger came out with a bag of meat.

On investigation, we found the fridge door shut. He also used to get bags of meat out of the freezer at the top of the fridge.

Apart from that one time, he always closed the workshop door behind him.

A LITTLE LEG-LIFTING

Mike Hayes

At dog shows, they sometimes have a 'Dog Most Like Its Owner' category. It goes hand-in-hand with the Man's Best Friend Philosophy of dog-owning. Basically, without dogs, humans'd be ... well, just humans. This yarn outlines another memorable collision between the human and canine universes. The bare bones of the yarn come initially from that inveterate tale-teller, Matt Crowe, whose memorable wine bar in the little village of Gundaroo, New South Wales, has been mentioned in my despatches before. Like most of Matt's yarns, I can't vouch for every detail. All I can say is that the people involved exist and if things didn't actually happen this way—they should have.

I reckon there are two things in life which come under the heading 'A Total Bloody Waste of Time' and that's politics and trying to work out which breed of sheepdog's the best! Looking back, if a bloke had to pick one particularly wasted afternoon out of an otherwise fruitful existence, it'd have to be that Election Day down the Dag Butterers' Arms. No, I can't quite remember which year it was, but it was quite a few Momentous Democratic Decisions ago.

Elections—whether they be Federal, State, Local Council or even Pastures Protection Board—tend to follow a seemingly ageless pattern in the bush. I don't mean the outcomes although, God knows, they always seem to be fairly predictable. What I mean is more the time-honoured drama that unfolds as the locals drift in to cast their votes.

For instance, back in those days, you could bet your boots the Back Creek brothers'd be the first into town to vote. Just like every bush town usually has a 'back creek' and therefore a Back Creek Road, they probably all have an equivalent of the Back Creek Brothers. What probably set our two apart from the rest is that you'd only ever see Vin and Doug in town together on polling days. Doug you'd rarely see in town at all.

They reckon he had a crook back from a lifetime of toiling away in shearing sheds or along fence lines, and couldn't work anymore. Like a lot of bushmen, he was scared stiff of doctors and hospitals and never did much about his back apart from half a lifetime of intensive Penfold's Therapy—trying to kill the agony with frequent applications of fortified wine. In between flagons, he kept to his bed for weeks on end. That's why it was always an experience to see him on Election Day. It wasn't an experience you'd quickly forget, either.

Vin, on the other hand, would breeze into town from their little slab shanty every few days to check their box at the post office and maybe pick up one or two essential domestic items such as food. According to local legend, on each trip Vin would stock up their larder with two meat pies.

'He takes 'em home, cuts 'em into four and they have a quarter each, once a day. That does 'em for tucker,' my informant (usually grossly unreliable) swears. It may or may not have been true. Both brothers looked like they hung from coat-hangers, rather than walked, so perhaps that's all they needed to keep them going.

Vin and Doug were drunks of the old school. Remember back in the old days, before people who indulged in a bit of excess kidney-flushing were said to have had Alcohol Related Problems? Drunks were just drunks—somewhat larger-than-life bods most notable, in small country towns after closing time, for being able to walk sideways while wheeling a bicycle. Drunks also used to sing a lot. Vin and Doug still did, especially on Election Day.

Drunks also used to argue. Vin and Doug still did, even more so on Election Day. Between them they exercised what you'd call Division of Labour. Vin performed the vocals, Doug starred in debating. Doug was what you'd call a Bar Clearer. He could involve a total stranger in a passionate argument on the most obscure subjects and within minutes have everyone else in the place hurriedly gulping down their port and lemonades and suddenly finding excuses to leave early. And that's how it went on that Election Day back in 19 . . . whenever it was.

About mid-morning, when most other early voters had been driven home by Doug's invective, poor old Harvey Drench came barrelling along in his old ute, with a team of motley sheepdogs, some of them vaguely resembling kelpies, chortling in the back. Harvey had been up to the school to vote and, like all other civic-minded electors, had called in for a quiet heart-starter before going about his normal, more productive business. (Harvey was in fact a chicken sexer and part-time crutcher . . . both pursuits eminently more worthwhile than voting).

It must have been the unseasonably warm weather, or something, but unlike the other early starters, Harvey was silly enough to actually become involved in conversation with Doug. Vin, just for the record, was sitting innocently on a stool under the hookey board, quietly crooning old half-remembered Tex Morton ballads to himself. Using hindsight, I suppose the subject under discussion would have been pretty predictable, considering the mutts bouncing about in the stock crate of Harvey's ute, harmonising closely with Vin's warbling.

'They're noisy bloody dogs, you've got there,' Doug observed belligerently.

'Aww! They're just itchin' to get going. We've got to move a big mob of sheep for a bloke up at Starpost,' replied Harvey, enjoying the first caress of Stone's Green Ginger Wine around his tonsils too much to realise that he'd taken a bait.

'Some of them look like kelpies,' Doug continued, closing one eye to focus a little better. He was obviously still feeling, not quite believing, his good luck in actually fluking someone prepared to discuss the subject further with him.

'Yup. Most of them blokes are out of that little red bitch there. Bought her up in Armidale. Best bloody working dogs in the world.'

Doug knew which line of attack he should take now! His reaction to Harvey's claim about his kelpies produced a look like the one Doug could well deliver if someone had spat into his glass. Off they went.

Doug suddenly developed an intense hatred of kelpies and started waxing lyrical about all their aberrations . . . which basically added up to the fact that they weren't worth a pinch of what-he-said compared with his own personal collection of prize collies.

Like I said, Harvey's brain mustn't have been functioning properly, because he waded in and decided to defend his mutts. A few other voters who'd stopped by began to deliver their

70

excuses most emphatically and moved towards the door.

'See ya later. Gotta take the kids to footie.'

'I'll see youse blokes around. The Missus'll be worrying where I am.'

'I'll be goin' too, fellers. Me mother-in-law's coming to visit and I'd like to be there to greet her.'

Although Jeff behind the bar looked as if he, too, would like nothing better than to go and greet his mother-in-law—or anyone else's for that matter—he abided by the ethics of his noble, self-sacrificing profession and chose to stay on and keep Doug and Harvey's glasses brimming, just in case they suddenly dehydrated. Over under the hookey board, Vin changed from Tex Morton to Buddy Williams with the vocal dexterity of a 'Julio Inglese'.

It went on all day. Voters came, drank briefly and fled, but still the argument continued.

'Bloody kelpies. They're gutless. A kelpie won't take on a big wether. They just drop to their bloody bellies and cringe.'

'Bull! A bloody collie just gives up and pisses off. And they get nasty when they get older. You find a sheep killer and you can bet it's a flamin' collie that don't know the difference between that and honest work.'

'Honest work? On a hot day, a bloody kelpie's just as likely to leave you halfway across the paddock and go for a swim in a bloody water trough.'

By late afternoon, even Jeff the publican was starting to flag. He sat in a corner, just ticking up the tab as the two contenders helped themselves from a bottle on the bar. After a Violet Crumble Bar health lunch, old Vinnie had abandoned his repertoire of Chad Morgan favourites and had dropped off.

There must have been a sudden wind change, or something, because all of a sudden, Harvey, who wasn't exactly spot-on in the sobriety stakes by then, suddenly seemed to come to his senses. While Doug spouted more anti-kelpie abuse to a couple more incautious souls who'd ventured into the bar, Harvey suddenly placed his glass firmly on the counter and tottered out to his ute where even his dogs, uncharacteristically quiet, showed signs of mental exhaustion. Rummaging around under the driver's seat, he careened back in, carrying a tiny red kelpie pup, about six weeks old.

71

'Here, Doug,' he intoned slowly and deliberately, 'I've heard so much balderdash from you on how bloody good your collies are, I reckon it's time you put your money where your mouth is. Take this pup—it's out of me good bitch—and bring it up like you do your precious collies. Feed it, train it and then see how it turns out. If it isn't ten times better than your dogs, I'll go He.'

Harvey's surprisingly generous gesture apparently struck a chord with Doug. Gently taking the pup from his opponent, he cradled it in his gnarled hands and actually started snivelling.

'Jesus. That's a decent thing to do, Drenchy. You're a reasonable sort of bloke—apart from your poor taste in dogs.'

And off they went again, hammer and tongs, Harvey defending his bitch's honour and Doug vitriolically predicting how useless the pup would be, despite the prospect of it enjoying the most expert training available in the land. He needed both hands to gesticulate and threaten violence with (not to mention emptying the occasional glass down the throat), so he stuffed the dozy little pup down his flannel singlet. After a couple of minutes the little bloke stopped wriggling and complaining and dropped off to sleep in the cosy warmth just above Doug's spare tyre.

Now, those of you who've taken a cold drink or two on festive occasions will be aware that prolonged sessions tend to put something of a strain on one's renal system. That certainly proved the case with Doug who suddenly felt an urgent need to empty his bladder.

'Hang on,' he belched to Harvey. 'I'll be back in a sec. I just wanna go out for a quick slash.'

For a waste disposal system as abused as Doug's, the hike out the back to the Gents' had always been a fairly ambitious project. Being an old hand at such personal crises, Doug knew better than to attempt it. There was hardly anyone around at that late hour (it was almost dark), so he floated out the front door onto the verandah for a quick piddle into the deserted main street.

Breathing in great lungfuls of fresh air as though close to nine hours of steady wading through four or five bottles of Mind Stealer had made him forget what it was like, Doug looked blearily at the distant hills, unzipped his fly and prepared to do what he had to do.

Engrossed in drinking in the wonders of the evening (while trying hard to maintain his equilibrium), he pulled out one of the forgotten pup's front legs and eased the strain on his bladder. Naturally, it wasn't too long before he started feeling distinctly uncomfortable. The discomfort became so intense that Doug was moved to look down to investigate its source.

It must have given him the shock of his life. A minute or two later, a pale-faced Doug came back into the bar, stone cold sober. He didn't say much, just something about growing claws in a funny place. And he didn't finish his drink. He just pushed his glass towards Jeff, gently shook Vin awake and helped him out into the dusk towards some spot further along the main street where they'd tethered their ute earlier in the day. It took a while for the full story to filter through to the rest of us.

'I bet that'll put the old bugger off the grog once and for all,' someone observed.

But it didn't, you know. He just gave up voting.

THE CAMP PIE TIN

J Woolford, Murray Town

My cousin offered me a brown kelpie named Peter. When I asked if he was any good, my cousin said, 'Too right! Whenever we throw out a camp pie tin, he goes out and rounds up the sheep.'

I hope the younger generations know what camp pie is. It was the greatest stand-by in the cupboard before refrigeration. We used it whenever there was no fresh meat. The dog was very good, and gave me many years of service.

PART 5

ALL IN THE LINE
OF DUTY

They won't just stick to sheep work either. They'll round up chooks, do a spot of nursing, ringbark trees, save humans, face the terrors of motorbikes and storms, not to mention getting shot on the job. . .all in the line of duty.

SUNDAY SINNER

Mike Hayes

It's a sad fact of life that working dogs, once described to me by an old-timer as the 'greatest source of free labour we've got', don't really spend an idyllic lifetime loping in slow motion through the long grass on sun-drenched fields. Out bush a great many of them lead miserable existences. The old tropical saying 'A dog, a woman, a mango tree—the more you beat them, the better they be' is adhered to far too strongly throughout rural Australia.

Oh sure, it's rarely deliberate, malicious cruelty. As far as the dogs go, it's more an odd philosophy declaring that if you treat your four-legged workmates too kindly, they'll go soft on you. The blokes who spout it will usually be, as they speak, fondling a tubby, wriggling puppy in their gnarled hands. If you regard the bushman's relationship with his dog as a working partnership, their often brutal attitude can perhaps be explained, but not necessarily excused, by recognising that bush life is just as hard on people as it is on dogs.

If anyone's aware of the place they personally hold in Australia's heritage, it's the people up in the Snowy Mountains. It hasn't been easy to hang onto it, either. In the late 1960s, the mountain people lost what they regarded as their inalienable right—ready access to the spectacular high country where they'd grazed their herds for generations. The legislation and official restrictions which accompanied the creation of the Kosciusko National Park not only prevented them taking their stock up there any more—it physically cut them off from the places they felt set them apart from the lesser mortals of the flat country. Those soul-stirring high plains had been as much a part of their being as the genes they inherited from the hardy pioneers who first trickled into the area in the 1840s and dotted the flats with their slab and bark huts, hoping to shelter their tough families from the savage blizzards that whip the mountains between April and October.

These days the mountain people grumble bitterly about losing the right to ride freely into the high country to lose themselves in its magic like they did in the old days. They'll mutter grimly about not being able to fatten their stock anymore in the fragile environment of the mountain pastures: 'We were up there for yonks. If anyone knows how to protect the flamin' environment, it's us!'

But deep down, you get the feeling that aspect doesn't worry them a fraction as much as just not being able to wander at will in the secluded places they once called their own. If they really wanted to go back up there, they could, although they'd have to swap the rolled swags, elastic-sided boots and stocky mountain ponies of old for backpacks, sneakers and ideologically sound bicycles. They don't bother.

The mountain people these days have accepted that stock work is no longer the honest livelihood it once was. Relatively few still farm seriously or profitably. Instead, you find the descendants of one branch of a pioneering family negotiating real estate deals with trendy yuppies anxious for a toehold close to the snowfields. Young people jangle cash registers in local supermarkets, peer from behind bank counters or pursue their studies in far-off Sydney. Only a dwindling number of old-timers still cling to the pioneer style of living. You reach their modest fibro homesteads along winding, rutted roads, shuttered off from the outside world by hard-to-open, twisted steel gates.

They've not changed. Nor have their dogs. As is the case throughout the bush, the first sign of life the visitor encounters is the assortment of canine workers bouncing enthusiastically at the end of their chains in front of their oil drum and hollow log kennels scattered around the higher points of the home paddock out of flood reach. The mountain people always let their dogs have their say before emerging from their own kennels, leaning cautiously on their gates until they work out who the hell you are.

Like their owners, a lot of the old dogs have seen better days. Most are in semi-retirement, let off occasionally to help round up the killers or maybe being allowed to pile squabbling into the back of the ute to check the pregnant ewes somewhere up the back paddock. They're kept more out of habit than for any firm husbandry reason.

Like all bushmen, the old mountain stockmen talk tough about their dogs: 'What that useless bugger needs is half an ounce of lead—fair between the eyes!' But all of them seem to hang onto old mates and not entirely for sentimental reasons. Those old dogs, like the clapped-out old nags dozing under the willows along the creek, are living reminders of another, freer, wilder time.

'First thing I do in the morning is come out here and check under the tank to see if old Caesar's still with us,' rumbles the old-timer, limping painfully over to the stand and squinting into the gloom. Caesar, bony and proppy in the rear, stiff with arthritis, his ears patchy and misshapen and his frosted muzzle grizzled and moist like his owner's, staggers out, his skinny tail moving ever so slightly and his eyes bleary in the sudden light.

'Shoulda put him down years ago. Just couldn't bring meself to do it.'

A cross bred pup appears from nowhere and bulldozes its way through our legs to bounce cheekily in front of Caesar. The old dog barely moves, but dispatches the upstart with a low, bubbly snarl and promise of a nip. The bewildered pup, glancing fearfully over his shoulder, scoots back to the safety of the sheds, his feelings badly wounded. Caesar creeps back to the comfort of his wheatbags under the tank stand.

'Funny thing about a real good dog like Caesar,' observes his owner, 'none of his offspring were ever any good. Mad as cut snakes.'

By the time we make off for the house, Caesar's head's on his paws again and he's drifted away, back to the dreamy days when he could shoot like an arrow across a paddock, turn a thundering mob and slot them neatly into any yards you'd nominate.

'I just let him keep going. So long as he's not in too much pain, I'll just let him be,' explains the boss, almost apologetically. 'Y'know, on a warm day, he'll still do his rounds. He checks all his favourite spots round the sheds and up the hill. Only difference these days is that it takes him all day to do it. And he sleeps for the next three to recover.'

Caesar actually represents the old bloke's own mortality. You can't escape the impression that the morning he checks under the tank and finds the old dog still and stiff in the frost, he'll turn around and seriously consider packing it in himself. But for now, Caesar and the other dogs are still part of his well-established lifestyle. Perhaps in the Jindabyne pub, or around the relative sophistication of a barbecue fire at a local property, he and the other old-timers will continue to swap stories about the dogs—good and bad—they've all owned at one time or another.

'You know what it's like,' Lanky Cauldron once explained, 'you get into a session like that and soon it's one bloke shouts a round . . . another bloke tells his dog yarns.

A mob of them were stuck one night like that down at the Snow Goose in Adaminaby. It was Dan Trembath's turn to shout and fate gave Lew Fletcher a turn at spinning a dog story.

'The only thing Lew and I agreed about was that I'd never been able to breed a decent dog myself,' Lanky recalled morosely. 'I never really knew whether his had been good or bad.'

Lew, on the other hand, had few qualms about the excellence of his personal mutts. To make his point, he started reminiscing about the time just about every able-bodied bloke in the mountains had headed up to Snowy Plain for the annual pre-winter muster. They pressed their luck a bit. They'd mustered most of the sheep—about 5000 of them—but still had another 800 to go, when the weather closed in. The ominous sky, which had been darkening all afternoon, seemed to lower over the alps. It would snow like buggery once it got dark. You could almost hear the temperature drop. There wasn't much wind at first. In fact, when the first snowflakes started to dance in front of the stockmen's eyes, conditions were deceptively calm. The musterers huddled inside the hut for a quick conference. It'd be too easy to get caught if a fully-blown blizzard moved in.

After they got together in the hut it didn't take long for the wind to join in the game and the flakes were soon hissing evilly against the draughty walls. It was then, according to his own account, that Lew came up with the perfect solution.

'I told them I had a bloody good dog with me and if they hung around and concentrated on finding the missing 800, I'd pick up the bulk of the mob and move them down the mountain out of the snow to the stock reserve. Me and that dog kept 'em together nicely. In fact, once we'd moved them off the moutain, things weren't too bad.'

It's like that in the high country. A blizzard can be snarling away at the top, but lower down it's mild and calm. Lew continued his saga while, over at the bar, Dan haggled with the barman about his change.

'It turned out to be a lovely, clear, moonlit night. In fact, it was so bright that after the dog and I got them to the reserve, we had enough light to count the mob. And guess what? They were all there.'

Dan juggled the round over and plonked the glasses onto the little table in front of the troops.

'Yep!' clucked Lew, taking a generous pull on his fresh beer, 'he was one hell of a dog.'

Solemnly, Dan raised his own glass and bellowed to the throng, 'Here's to Lew. From now on his name's changed. After a claim like that, Fletcher is officially known as Stretcher.'

And what about the mountain dogs who were so good in the yards, they could even do up the gates?

'You've heard the yarn, haven't you?' asked Lanky Cauldron, 'about the bloke who reckoned his dog was so smart that he could pen a mob of sheep, push the hurdle gate shut himself and even jump up and put in the little wooden peg to keep it shut? The only problem was that those little pegs had a habit of fallin' out and if that happened, the bloody sheep'd get out.'

Some other bloke, who'd been listening all night without saying much, suddenly snorted with contempt.

'Piss weak. Don'cha know anything? Round our way, we train dogs properly. Once they get the sheep in and the gate shut, they piddle on the little pegs, wait for the moisture to swell the wood, then they put the bloody things in. That way, they never bloody well fall out!'

But there were dogs whose ability no mountain man would ever question. Such a toiler was old Tom McGufficke's Sunday. His feats were frequently discussed, from back in the days when stockmen roasted their backs and fronts alternately against a roaring fire of twisted snowgum limbs, yarning away the long autumn evenings at the mustering camps. Nowadays, Sunday's

79

name is more likely to come up when the remnants of that same dashing band of riders reminisce quietly around a similar blaze in someone's Saturday night backyard, where the flickering flames allow them to relive those older, wilder times and where, for a moment at least, the ever-encroaching outside world stays hidden away in the darkness.

'Remember that time old Tom and some of the blokes got caught by the rain on their way to Corryong?'

McGufficke and the others were performing an annual chore, moving a big mob from the New South Wales side across the mountains and the Murray to Victoria. They'd moved most of the herd across the river when the weather broke. With the worst of the trip behind them, the mountain men might have been expected to shrug it off and continue on the relatively short leg to Corryong, but all of them were aware that some of the mob weren't accounted for.

The river, fed by the runoff from a whole night of rain, rose quickly, then leaked out a thousand brown fingers across the flats. Daylight showed their instincts had been right. In the middle of the rushing flood, a sorry band of cattle could be made out stranded on a temporary island a couple of hundred yards from the main mob. Tom McGufficke decided it was indeed a job for Sunday.

He didn't need to explain too much to the dog. Sunday threw himself enthusiastically into the torrent and was soon reduced to a small black dot, heading determinedly across the muddy ocean. Eventually he pulled himself from the water on the island, paused for a few seconds to shake the excess from his coat and then hurtled forward to do the job required. The cattle didn't argue with Sunday. He soon coaxed them into the floodwaters, then plunged in behind them and didn't let up until he'd headed them in the right direction, straight over to the Victorian side. As the exhausted cattle finally dragged themselves to safety, they were expertly picked up by a couple of the stockmen and driven over to where the rest of the mob waited in the drizzle.

'Hey, Tom,' someone called. 'Where's Sunday? Is he with you?'

McGufficke checked quickly around him, but there was no dark shadow trotting quietly behind him. A wider check showed no dark form resting awhile in the shelter of the river gums. A few more hurried checks with the other drovers and it soon became apparent that Sunday was no longer with them.

The cattle had started moving off southwards of their own accord and the stockmen couldn't hang around for long. They dallied as long as they dared, all of them avoiding the boss's gaze as they looked in vain for some sign of their brave little mate.

'Well, that's it then,' McGufficke sighed finally. 'The poor bugger's gone down in the line of duty.'

'He was a pretty good dog, though,' someone muttered before they all wheeled their mounts and took up their positions for the last leg of the drive.

It took a few more days to get rid of the mob in Corryong and spend some time propping up a bar or two, swapping a few yarns with mates they hadn't sighted since last year, before the mountain men turned their horses' heads towards home. It wasn't too long, however, before word got around that old Tom had received the surprise of his life when he leant from his saddle to open the last gate into Leesville—and was greeted with great familiarity by Sunday.

'Jesus, Tom, you musta been glad to see him. What did'ja do?' someone asked him when he recounted the incident later in the old Jindabyne pub.

'I gave the old bastard the biggest hiding of his life,' Tom muttered. 'That'll teach him to bloody well leave me like that.'

As Lanky philosophised: 'It didn't matter that old Sunday had swum the flooded Murray and crossed the alps just to get home. You expect that from a good dog. But you never expect him to shoot through on you.'

A BIT OF A SHOW-OFF

Max Nitschke, Keith

Most dogs work for just one master. If anyone else tries to reproduce the commands they know, or tries to give them a task, they usually react with disdain—and go off and lie under a tree. Sometimes, they'll just be confused and not understand what it is that another is trying to tell them to do. So it's an unusual dog that will work for absolutely anybody.

Enter Trixie, who was used by all the neighbours in the Marcollat district in the south-east of South Australia whenever they had something their own dogs couldn't handle. At lamb-marking time, she was particularly sought after. Lambs are difficult to control because they tend to run blindly in all directions. It takes a special kind of dog to keep calm with lambs and not rush them. So they called in Trixie.

But she was good with everything. In fact she was a bit of a show-off. At shearing time, when all the sheep were penned up and she didn't have anything to do, she would come down to the house and work on the white rooster. Whether, because of his colour, she thought he needed shearing too, no-one knows. But she would separate him from the hens and nose him right up to the shearing shed, then inside the door—much to his displeasure. The old rooster would be cackling with annoyance and the shearers and everyone in the shed would laugh.

This dog would not only work anything on the ground, she was also a good retriever in the water at duck-shooting time. She'd swim out, half stand up in the water to get her bearings, then grab the duck. If it was still alive and it dived, she'd go underwater after it, then swim back with it in her mouth and drop it at my feet. She was better than any Labrador.

She'd also do her sheep work under remote control. I could stand here on the front verandah and send her out to the far paddock to bring in a mob. She'd go out in the direction I pointed, then at a certain distance look back for further instructions. If she couldn't see me clearly, she'd stand up on her hind legs for a better view. If she still couldn't see my hand signals clearly, I'd use a long stick. Whichever side I was pointing to, she'd go until she found the mob and brought them right back in.

I also used to start her off with a mob of ewes and lambs that I was sending to market. They'd be in a paddock about two miles from the yards, and they are really slow to move because the lambs get separated from their mothers and the mothers fuss around. Anyway, it would get to smoko time, and I'd feel like a cuppa, so I'd leave Trixie to carry on alone. When I got back to her, she'd still have every sheep and would be a good half mile closer to the yards. She would never leave any behind because she would only go the pace of the slowest sheep. Too many dogs will push them and make them scatter.

Trixie was a border collie, and I must have had her thirteen or fourteen years. I've had kelpies, but I always reckon border collies have a few more brains. I didn't have to teach her anything. It was sort of born in her. She started work when she was three months old, and was nearly a professional straight away. As a pup, she worked like an old dog, and she was just as good in the yards as she was in the paddock.

I really missed Trixie when she was gone. You only get about three good dogs in a lifetime. She was gentle and good with kids, but tough. With her son, she'd kill kangaroos when it was time to stock up on dogs' meat. They'd jump off the ute when we came across a big scrubber. Those big scrubbers don't run very far—only about 100 yards and then they sit up— but they'll fight. Those two dogs would catch them and kill them every time, and never get hurt.

They worked as a team. One would goad him in front, and the other would go and give him a bite on the bum. When he was turning around, the other would go in and give him a bite. This would go on for a fair while, then when they got tired, they'd lie down in a pool of water for ten minutes and have a good spell.

Then they'd both get up and start working on the roo again, until eventually the old kangaroo would tip over. Then they'd go and give him a bite in the throat. Yet they were never dogs that would hurt sheep. In those early days, there were plenty of kangaroos, and you fed your dogs on them.

I reckon those days were especially good for dogs. It was fairly wet here and you couldn't get out in a vehicle. If you wanted a mob of sheep in, you walked. While you walked, you could train a dog and the dog could hear everything you said. Since I've had motorbikes, I've had nowhere near as good dogs. Bikes are so noisy and we rush and tear around with the dogs on the back yapping and barking. I miss old Trix, and those days.

DOWN THE BLOWHOLE

DC McCracken, Elliston

My late uncle once owned, amongst his various sheepdogs, a small black and grey bitch named Winnie.

Winnie was absolutely sheep-obsessed. She would become excited at the mere mention of the animals.

On one occasion, when mustering with her master, who was on horseback, she came back to him in a very agitated state. She indicated that she wanted him to follow her.

He eventually did and she led him some distance away to a limestone blowhole several feet deep. Down it was a sheep.

The sheep was rescued unharmed and Winnie returned to her mustering duties with an air of self-satisfaction and relief.

THE FOX HUNTER

Joy Nunan, Port Pirie

My story is over thirty-five years old. We were living on a mixed farm and my father used to breed fat lambs for export. The foxes were bad. They tortured and killed many baby lambs. To combat them, he used to poison them and go spotlighting.

One day, a young dog came to our place. We were unable to find his owner, so he stayed. Quite a good worker he was too. He also loved spotlighting and became excited as soon as we picked up the gun.

The problem with him, though, was once a fox was sighted, we were unable to keep him on the truck with us. We lost several of the distant foxes that he was unable to run down. He would jump on top of the near ones and roll over. My father would have to shoot the fox as it lay under the dog. After the fox had been shot, the proud laugh on the face of that dog was a sight to behold.

Knowing the law of averages, however, my father realised the dog would have to stay home. He was tied up on a hefty farm chain. The next time we went shooting, it was without Mickey and consequently there was not quite the usual amount of excitement.

We duly rounded up our fox. Believing Mickey was safely at home at the end of his chain, my father pulled the trigger.

I don't remember what happened to the fox, but it seems Mickey had broken the chain and was just outside the spotlight. He collected some of the shot in his front leg.

These days, he could have been saved, but thirty-five years ago, I do not know if the expertise was available. Even so, there was not enough money available to take 'just a dog' to the vet. So, a few days later, to relieve his suffering, Dad shot him. We were all very sad and missed him terribly. I guess it must have hurt my father the most as that was the second time that he had had to put down his favourite dog.

THE CASANOVA CHAINSAW

Mike Hill, Cape Jervis

We were short of dogs on the farm in 1966, so for $40 I bought Ringo and a bitch from Cec O'Leary, one of the local characters. Cec's parting words to me when I collected the dogs were, 'If ever you want to get sheep out of a gully, say to Ringo 'Go get 'em'. Then he'll run to the nearest tree, jump up and grab a low-hanging limb with his teeth, swing in the air and make funny howling noises. The sheep will then get out of the gully.'

Cec was a good yarn-spinner, so I laughed and told him to pull the other leg.

Anyway, one day I had a pile of sheep that I had to get out of a particularly steep gully. I had been trying to move them for a while with no success. I remembered Cec's words. When I checked no-one was looking, I gave the command. 'Go, get 'em, Ringo'.

Sure enough, to my open-mouthed surprise, Ringo ran up to the nearest tree, grabbed hold of a branch and swung there, letting out blood-curdling noises. The sheep were so terrified, they bolted out of the gully.

Because no-one ever believed me when I later told this story, we have recorded Ringo doing his trapeze act on film. Apart from that one peculiar working method, Ringo was a perfectly normal dog. A big border collie cross with longish hair, he was in fact a very good worker.

However, he had a couple of personal habits which I suppose could be called faults. He loved wood. The tree-swinging trick was, I suppose, a part of this affinity with wood, but it went further than that. He had a compulsive desire to ringbark trees. Whenever he had a spare minute, he'd be out in the paddock stripping bark off trees from the ground to as high as he could reach. He loved the stringy-barks and would pull great long

86

strips off. It was a common sight to see him hard at work, being urged on by two of his favourite bitches barking excitedly. You could always tell where he'd been by the piles of bark at the base of every tree. He killed hundreds of trees, something I'm not the slightest bit proud of. This environmentally damaging habit caused him to be banned from nearly every farm in the district.

Ringo even ate the whole front out of his kennel, so that the roof collapsed. After that, he used to lie on the roof. He completely wore his teeth out. They were just tiny white stumps by the end of his life.

All of his pups, and there were an awful lot of them in the district, but I'm coming to that, had the same destructive habit. People put up with them, though, because they were excellent workers. But it did get to the stage where we ran out of homes for the pups. So we used to take them to pet shops in the city. One day, not long after having delivered a litter, I was listening to a talkback programme on the radio. An irate woman came on. She said she had just bought a pup from a city pet shop.

'People should vet these dogs,' she said. 'My pup's just ringbarked all my trees.' I suppose I shouldn't have laughed. But it had to be one of old Ringo's pups.

By now you are wondering why we allowed this renegade dog to wander the district chomping through trees and siring pups everywhere. The truth is, he was impossible to tie up. We used to tighten his collar until his eyes bulged, but he had a thick neck and smallish head in comparison, and he would just slip his collar every time. You would just finish tying him up, feeling as though you were cruel making the collar so tight, and be walking to the ute. He'd be right behind you before you had even reached the vehicle. We would lock him up in a shed, but he would chew his way through the door. He had teeth like a chainsaw.

The other undesirable characteristic of Ringo was that he was a sex maniac. We lived on the top of a range of hills which flattened out and ran down to the sea. Ringo's beat extended down to the coast, along the hills and almost to the local town— a good five miles in all directions. Within that radius, he took it upon himself to service every on-heat bitch.

Every litter of pups born during his lifetime had the unmistakable stamp of Ringo. Other male dogs would stand aside when Ringo appeared, and let him go about his business. He was so notorious as a seducer of females that farmers would lock up their bitches when they were on heat behind thick doors. This didn't worry old chainsaw Ringo. He'd be through the door in a flash.

One day a bloke rang me to say he'd caught Ringo hanging around his bitch and that he had locked him in a shed and nailed a piece of weldmesh in front of the door.

'It couldn't be Ringo,' I said. 'He's asleep on the verandah. I can see him.'

The poor bloke went to check his shed. Ringo had eaten through the door above where the weldmesh stopped—about three feet up.

I wasn't one of the most popular blokes in the district. Understandably, sheep men got pretty sick of their working bitches always being pregnant, so they'd take a gun to him. Time and time again, he came home with buckshot up his arse. That would quieten him down for a while. But after we had picked out the shot and the wounds had healed, he'd be at it again.

Eventually, he was peppered with a bit too much lead. He developed a hernia in his rear, and became too sick to go on his visits. He would lie in his hollow under the house and sleep.

Every now and again, though, we would hear a lot of barking and scuffling from Ringo's pad. We'd go down and have a look, and there would be old Ringo, hard at it. Because he was too injured to travel to his girls, they came to him. They would arrive two at a time and he would dutifully deal with them, before watching them trot off out the gate again.

He died of his injuries at the age of twelve.

A STRAY SAVIOUR

Kate Heron, Kimba

This is a true story told to me by my grandfather. The morning was calm and warm. It would be pretty hot before the day was through, the boy told his pony as he fixed the slip rails behind the cows he had just yarded.

He must hurry. His pony had to have breakfast and so did he before he rode to school. Suddenly he saw a black and white dog out on the flat. He went over towards it, calling gently, but the dog withdrew into the scrub.

The property already had three sheepdogs, so it was only to be expected that the boy's father did not greet the news of a stray dog with any enthusiasm. He merely commented that an eye would have to be kept on the sheep in case the dog got too hungry.

Two mornings later, the dog appeared again, lying half a mile away on the flat. The boy again called softly and gently to the dog. This time, the dog began to crawl towards the boy on its stomach whimpering as it came. Five yards away, it stopped. The boy didn't move. He just kept talking softly, with his hand outstretched. With a quick wriggle, the dog put its head under the outstretched hand.

That began an inseparable friendship that lasted as long as the dog. After a great deal of persuasion, the boy's father said the dog could be kept—especially after he discovered the dog would work sheep and cattle equally well. Nobody ever claimed the dog.

During the Depression years, many farmers had been forced to leave their properties and find work in other areas, such as Whyalla, then a boom town. It was later discovered that the dog's original owner was one such family, but the dog hadn't settled into city life. When he returned to his old home, he had found it deserted. Hunger and thirst had forced him to move from farm to farm only to be hunted on until he arrived at Yeltana.

The dog was named Mukksy after a murderer who killed a taxi driver, shortly before the dog did the same with several chickens. Although he was not permitted to go to school, Mukksy would set off each afternoon, regardless of the weather, to meet the boy on his way home. At thirteen, the boy left school to work at Buckleboo Station. He took the dog with him.

One day he was mustering straggler sheep with the manager when he hit the limb of a tree at full gallop and was swept from his horse. The manager did not notice the boy's disappearance until much later. It was near sunset when the dog, which until then had been keeping flies away from the boy, left.

When the dog joined Mr Miller, who had been droving the sheep they had found that day, it seemed so agitated that Mr Miller realised something was wrong. The manager hadn't seen the lad either, and they both knew the dog normally wouldn't go anywhere without him.

Mr Miller left the sheep and began to follow Mukksy who raced off in the direction of the injured boy. It was almost dark and mid-winter.

It is doubtful if the boy would have survived the night if he hadn't been found.

This boy was my grandfather—and he still loves his dogs more than his wife.

THE EYE OF THE STORM

Syd Nosworthy, Lucindale

When Ray Nosworthy set out to muster a remote property, he followed a well-established routine. He rode to the mustering hut, dropped some food and went on with his kelpie bitch, Brownie, to muster the sheep.

Having scoured the big paddock, he started the mob for the hut. The routine was to place the mob in a section of fenced laneway, string wire across the mouth and spend the night in the hut ready to resume the journey next morning.

All had gone smoothly—until mid-afternoon. Brownie gave the first indication of trouble. Like many dogs, she was afraid of storms and Ray noticed she was tending to abandon her normal role of trotting slowly at the rear of the mob. While still keeping the sheep headed in the right direction, she kept returning to the proximity of the horse.

The reason was soon apparent. The skies darkened and before long thunder could be heard. Lightning and thunder coming ever closer were obviously disturbing the dog but with the hut in sight, Ray thought he would get the mob safely in the lane.

However, the leaden skies brought on premature darkness and at the same time rain began to fall. And how it rained. Great gusts of water, cascading down, reduced visibility in short order from yards to nil. In the frequent lightning flashes, Ray saw that the sheep had broken and scattered. He could not see the dog and his calls were drowned in the wild rolls of thunder and the drumming of the pelting rain.

Abandoning the sheep, he rode to the hut expecting to find Brownie already cowering there. She wasn't. He turned his horse loose, lit the old lantern in the hut and called. There was no response. Leaving the lantern in the doorway to attract the dog's attention, he lit a roaring fire, stripped off his sodden clothes and strung them up to dry. After a meal, he still could not attract Brownie, so he reluctantly gave up and climbed into the bunk. The storm was still raging and the rain was unceasing. He was up at first light. The storm had passed but he could see in its wake great sheets of water across the flat landscape.

Saddling his horse, he could see knots of sheep on high ground in the lane. Approaching he could see that all the sheep seemed to be in the lane on the higher ground—a subsequent count revealed they were all there. His surprise did not last long. As he neared the mouth of the lane, he saw Brownie, half submerged in water, patiently watching the lane to see no sheep wandered out.

He could only marvel firstly at her skill in getting the sheep into the lane and the amazing devotion she showed to her task by spending the night in conditions she found completely terrifying. When he reached her, she could scarcely move. Shivering and stiff, she had obviously remained at her post for hours. Knowing the sheep were not likely to escape through the water, Ray picked up the dog and carried her on the saddle to the hut.

Brownie was put in front of the re-activated fire and gradually thawed out. She ate a few scraps and appeared to be ready to work. The rest of the journey was across high ground and the sheep were in their paddock by about midday.

It was soon obvious that Brownie had not escaped the ordeal unscathed. She became listless and was patently ill. Ray carried her on the saddle until they reached home where he bedded her down. She was very sick for some time, but after patient nursing, recovered. It was not a complete recovery, however.

Brownie's lungs had suffered some damage and for the rest of her life, she wheezed and coughed with almost every movement. Although she learnt to canter for short distances, Ray realised she would never be able to work in the paddocks again. She became, instead, an honoured pensioner. But she wasn't keen on idle retirement, and wasn't happy.

However, Brownie was in luck. Ray's brother, Frank, suffered from a chronic heart condition that restricted him to walking pace only. He and Brownie fitted their lives together. She could yard the killers from a small paddock and she soon learnt to bring the cows in for milking twice a day.

Perhaps her most skilful function, though, was with the

chooks. Poultry in those days was still very much a luxury. Frank reared a large number of cockerels and kept the homestead, friends and relatives supplied. They were free-range birds and his problem was to catch them. Gathering the fowls with some wheat, he would lunge at the cockerel of his choice with a piece of wire.

Brownie picked up her cue at once. Circling the bird, she quickly closed on it, pushed it over with her nose, and without disturbing a feather, placed one paw on it and held it until Frank arrived to pick it up.

Hundreds of times over the years she carried out this task, without ever harming a bird.

THE RABBIT COLLECTOR

Mrs AM Cox, Carrieton

I cannot imagine life on the land without at least one or two sheepdogs about the place. Regardless of their value as workers (they are better than an extra man up in the rough country) they are really great companions. I am on my own and fairly isolated most days, so I appreciate having them sprawled on the lawn or the back doormat. This is my favourite story about a faithful worker we know.

Increasing rabbit numbers were causing concern on our property, so we spent our evenings shooting by spotlight. A friend offered his assistance which we gladly accepted as he was a good shot—an experienced fox shooter.

He arrived in his utility, which was equipped with safety bars, and also his dog—his constant companion.

After about three hours, we had reduced the rabbit population somewhat, and being frozen to the marrow, decided to return to the house for a warm-up by the fire and a hot drink. The rabbits were thrown in a heap on the back lawn to be dealt with later, and inside we went.

When we went out to farewell our friend, about an hour later, we found that his dear old dog had laboriously loaded every rabbit back onto his boss's ute—and was standing guard over them.

What a job! He had jumped down, picked up a carcass, jumped up and dropped it, then gone back down for another one. He had obviously decided that those rabbits belonged only to his boss.

AS GOOD AS ANY YARD

Dick Mills, Kanmantoo

I thought you may like to know that I once saw my cousin, Bruce Mills, bring in a mob of sheep using eight dogs together. Eight dogs! Usually one is enough trouble for the average sheepman. Bruce had his dogs bring in the sheep in order to catch one, but he did this in an open paddock, without the use of a yard.

This was no trouble for Bruce. He held the sheep against the fence with each dog sitting, evenly spaced, under perfect control in a semicircle around the sheep while he went in and caught one. The dogs were as good as any yard.

THE BANTAM'S REVENGE

Chris Collins, Meningie

Fred was my first sheepdog when I went away jackerooing. He was a sort of big, gallumphing, lumpish, black and white kelpie sheepdog—a bit clumsy, but he showed a fair bit of ingenuity right from the word go. I remember the manager at the station where I was working finally coming to me in absolute desperation one day.

'Look,' he said, 'you've got to do something about your dog. It's plucking all our chooks.'

And it was true. All the chooks were running around with no feathers on them. . .just bald chooks everywhere. They didn't like it much. They went off the lay.

He was just a pup at the time and tied up on a dog wire. He would grab the chooks as they came past, sit down with a chook between his paws and tear its feathers out. When it was suitably bald, he would put it down and look for the next one. He was quite quiet about it. He must have clamped his foot over their heads to stop them squawking. I never actually saw him doing it, but there were always feathers around his drum.

From that unpromising beginning, Fred actually went on to be a very good sheepdog. But it turned out that the chooks more or less got their revenge, through a poultry namesake in the shape of a motorbike.

Fred had come back with me to the family farm—I must have been about nineteen—and I'd bought my first motorbike. It was an old BSA Bantam and I paid thirty dollars for it. There wasn't room for a carrier on the back of it, so Fred used to sit on the petrol tank in front of me. I used to use it to go down to the other block which is about twenty miles away.

On a hot day, Fred would leap off the bike, jump into a trough and then get up in front of me. It wasn't bad—a hot day, and a wet dog in front of you. It was a bit of free air-conditioning. He got to the stage, though, where he didn't like motorbikes.

I had just done the bike up and it went pretty well. We were heading down the road, with old Fred all wet and dripping, and I was enjoying the cool blast of air. But then, his wet tail sort of crept over the side of the petrol tank and headed towards the engine. It made contact with the spark plugs. We were doing about fifty miles an hour down a dirt road. Fred sort of went all stiff and arched his back and leant against me. When he did that, I got a charge too. So there we were, old Fred and me, roaring along the road, both rigid. We ground ourselves to a halt on the side of the road and fell off the bike. It took a bit of coaching to get him back on it after that. He finally did.

In the meantime, I'd decided the old, fixed-seat on the bike was a bit rough, so I made up a frame and put a spring-action seat on the bike. It was off an old German motorbike and it pivotted at the front and had a couple of springs underneath. It moved as the bike moved underneath you.

So we finally got Fred on the bike again and with the new seat we headed out over the big veldt grass clods on the place. It was a bit rough and bumpy. I didn't realise it at the time, but as the seat was rocking up and down, the little gap between the petrol tank and the seat was opening up and closing. It went from about half an inch to about two inches, and then it would close again as I hit a bump. Well, a very delicate part of Fred's anatomy rattled down between the seat and the petrol tank. I can still see Fred now, with his cods caught between the tank and the seat. . .poor old Fred, he was galloping on the petrol tank, but he couldn't go anywhere until we hit the next bump, and it let him go.

I never, ever got Fred back on that bike again. He wouldn't go near it. For the rest of his life, he preferred to run.

PART 6

NINE LIVES

And they don't give up easily either. Country life can be pretty harsh and the dogs come in for their share—harsh conditions, harsh masters and terrible accidents. They seem to survive it all.

EVERY YEAR FOR THE REST OF HIS LIFE

Don Stevens, Port Lincoln

We lived on a farm in the foothills, and Toby used to get the cows in every morning when he heard my father's alarm go off at 5 am.

In the evening, when my mother took the basket to collect the eggs, he would, without being told, again go and collect the cows.

Being in the hills, Toby used to go to the highest point and then sit, looking all over the valleys and other hills until he saw where the cows were. Then he'd bring them in at a steady walk.

On one occasion, we had arrived home in the buggy from the Clare Show, thirty miles away. It was 10 o'clock at night. Father said he wouldn't bother about milking because of the time.

Toby met us and jumped up on the hub of the front wheel to greet us, and then he went over towards the cowyard.

Dad said, 'If that old bloke has the cows in, we will have to milk them for him.'

Sure enough, he had the cows in and was lying across the gate to keep them in.

One time, my mother, who hates snakes, was killing one on the front verandah. Toby hated snakes too and always killed them if he could. Mum growled at him and told him to keep away. In the instant that Toby's eyes flashed towards Mum, the snake must have bitten him. He killed it, but Mum didn't know he had been bitten until quite a while later when she went outside and found Toby prostrate.

Father was at the neighbour's place working the team. Mother rang and told the neighbour to tell Father that Toby had been bitten by a snake and to come home.

The neighbour went out to Father, waving and yelling, 'Go home. The baby has been bitten by a snake.'

Father unyoked the team and rode home on one horse, only to find out it was Toby, not the baby.

They searched through an old doctor's book for remedies for snake bite. One was: 'Strong black coffee—as strong as possible.' Father, using a spoon got some into Toby, who was by then unconscious.

Toby did survive but at the same time of the year, each year for the rest of his life, he was affected by that snakebite. He was unable to get up in the morning without being helped.

It got so bad that Toby would be down for several days before the effects of the bite wore off. Father finally had to put him down as he was a man who did not like to see animals suffer.

THE SAMOYED BITCH

Dr Ron Baker, Yankalilla

When I was working as a vet in a Victorian country town, I knew a farming couple who had a Samoyed bitch. They had owned her for quite a few years. They were a typically tough Aussie couple, dairy farmers, who were also pretty tough on their dogs. The dogs would be chained up to their 44-gallon drum kennels, chucked a few bones at night, and if they didn't work as they were meant to do, they copped a piece of 'four by two' over the head.

The Samoyed, although the daughter of a kelpie working bitch, looked almost pure Samoyed, her father's breed. Because she was pretty, she had been kept for the children to play with. She was silvery-white, long-haired, with a typical curling tail and lovely greeny-brown eyes. Only a few black flecks in her hair indicated she was not a pure-bred. I had been treating her on and off over the years for various things and had always liked her.

One night, I had a call from Jim, the dairyman.

'I want you to have a look at my dog,' he said. He sounded quite insistent. I arranged to meet him at the clinic.

Well, I was quite shocked. This once beautiful dog was a sad and sorry sight. Her hair was falling out. She was skinny and there was pus coming out of her vulva. I diagnosed her as having an infected uterus, and could treat her only by operating and without too much delay. Jim, however, said he wanted the dog put down. He said he had never liked the dog. The children were all in the car and were in tears, but he was insistent. 'Put it down,' he said.

I told him that for $150 I would be able to cure her. 'You've got plenty of money,' I said. 'Go on, she's a lovely dog.'

But Jim left the surgery with clear instructions that I had to put the dog down. I was terribly distressed. This dog had a beautiful nature, and I just didn't want to do it. So for the next five minutes, the Samoyed and I just sat looking at each other. I had tears in my eyes and, as true as I sit here talking, she had tears welling in her eyes.

I said to this dog, 'Look, I just can't put you down.'

I rang the senior vet in the practice and explained the situation: that despite being instructed to dispose of the dog, I couldn't. I asked him if I could spend some of his money and save it, and then find it a home. Definitely not, was his answer. The only way around it was to ask the owner if I could operate, and foot the bill myself.

I rang him and put that to him. He still said, 'No. Put the dog down.'

So I got the syringe out of the cupboard and filled it with Lethobarb, the euthanasia solution, to do the job. I sat down on the floor with the dog, the syringe in my hand, and we had a chat with each other for ten minutes, trying to talk through the problem. And that dog cried. It had tears running down its cheeks and was making sobbing noises. I am sure it knew what was going on. I cried too.

Suddenly, I stood up and thought, 'Blast it! I'm in this game because I care about animals.' So, I did the operation and thought, 'To hell with the consequences.' I saved the dog.

Extraordinarily, while I was in the midst of the operation, the wife of the dairyman rang and said they had reconsidered their decision and that I could go ahead, if I could find it a home. That was a relief as I wasn't sure how I was going to face the ethical problem of having disobeyed a client's instructions.

When the Samoyed recovered, I gave her to a sheep farmer who was a friend of mine who loved dogs and was happy to help out with a home.

Some months later he approached me, absolutely overjoyed. 'That dog is one of the best sheepdogs I have ever had,' he said. 'She's an eyeball dog, but she's good in the yards as well as the paddock. Thank you.'

She also had become the special companion of the sheep farmer's spastic grandson, who lived on the property, giving him special warmth and friendship to cope with his difficulties.

Whenever I visited that farm, that dog never forgot me. It was always very clear we had a very special bond. She knew I'd saved her.

BACK FROM THE DEAD

Denis Adams, Apsley

Taffy came into our family as a pet for our kids. Since we'd sold our farm, we had no need of sheepdogs and by no stretch of the imagination could anyone see Taffy as a sheepdog. His mother had been a Welsh corgi and his father an Australian

101

terrier. The result was a dumb, suspicious, grovelling, ginger-haired, yellow-eyed mutt. Every time he was let off the chain, he'd vanish, so in an attempt to cure his ways, I desexed him. This was a complete waste of time as it was not animal lust that lured him away from home, I discovered, but a compelling love of nature. It was the poetic, Welsh side of him coming out. What other dog will sit for an hour, admiring the play of light on a pool of water, or watch chickens for hours on end without a base motive? What other dog will paddle quietly about in a farm dam, his face aglow with pleasure as he watches baby ducks?

It got a bit lonely driving a tractor out in the pine forest, so I weakened and sometimes took Taffy with me. The pleasure proved to be his, rather than mine. His nuisance value outweighed any fleeting pleasure he gave me.

One day I was working scrub land up for pines, using a heavy plough with two rows of fearsome-looking serrated discs. It was almost inevitable, I suppose, for him to get run over. By the time I managed to stop, there was no sign of him—just a neat swathe of freshly-ploughed sand.

Then, as I watched, the sand stirred and a bewildered-looking dog rose out of it. He sat there awhile, swaying a little, with blood oozing from his ears and a dozen deep gashes in his body. One front foot had been cut in half, right down the middle, and I could see he had broken ribs. As to his internal injuries, I could only guess.

I had no gun with me and I could not bring myself to kill him with the back of my axe. I decided to wait until he began coughing blood, then there could be no further excuses. By some miracle, though, it seemed his lungs had avoided damage, so I rolled him in my jacket and took him home. After two weeks in bed, he had made a complete recovery without any help from vets.

During his illness, I noticed a great change come over our formerly dopey dog. He began showing gratitude when I brought him his invalid fare of bread and milk. It seemed the accident had triggered off some previously dormant part of his brain. Taffy rose from his sick-bed, a reformed character. He was suddenly a faithful, courageous and intelligent dog.

Overnight, he blossomed into a first-rate sheepdog. He

became a great hunter as well and was unafraid of dogs twice his size. He also seemed to have telepathic powers. On the day of the Ash Wednesday fires in the south-east, he began acting in a most peculiar way. An hour or two before the fire started, Taffy was terrified and began looking for places to hide. I remember asking him jokingly if there was something that he knew that no-one else did!

About three years ago, he decided that his race was run. He hadn't been well and was spending more and more time in bed. Finally, he only seemed to come out to eat and drink. The time seemed to have come for a replacement.

The new pup had hardly set foot in our yard before Taffy made another amazing recovery. From then on, if anyone paid the slightest attention to the pup, Taffy was on the scene, shouldering it aside to claim all the attention for himself.

Our battle-scarred old Taffy still soldiers on. He can still run, though no longer very fast nor far, and his left legs now seem to take longer strides than his right ones. But he's still going!

THE TWO-LEGGED BATTLER

C Gerschwitz, Minnipa

While showing signs of becoming a good working dog, Bob became the devoted and protective friend of Ann, our twelve-year-old daughter. Roaming the farm together, learning to swing on the swing, slide down the slippery-dip and ride with her on the motorbike were just some of the escapades of these two.

If Ann had a lolly, cake or ice-cream, there always had to be one for Bob as well.

Bob was a very ordinary black sheepdog of no special breeding. Due to his clumsiness, he gained broken leg number one at the age of six months. Using our bush first-aid, the leg was crudely set with bark and bandages. Daily, he chewed it off.

In desperation, we sought help, and the leg was set in plaster. Again, he chewed at it. To discourage this, we placed a pantihose leg over his head, exposing only his eyes and ears, and removed it only for him to eat. Callers at the farm found this very funny.

Broken leg number two came some weeks later when he overbalanced while riding on the back of the ute. We followed the same procedure, but it was a different leg.

Once recovered, he would watch for the school bus each afternoon at 4.30. Bob would then walk down to meet Ann, eat the remains of her school lunch and then have a race home. Ann rode her bike and Bob ran.

Eventually the time came for Ann to live in Adelaide to complete her schooling. The dog fretted at home and the child fretted in Adelaide. There was always a joyous reunion at holiday-time. However, the ritual of waiting for the school bus continued for many weeks. Bob would watch until the bus drove out of sight, then he would slink back home quite dejected.

He continued to be either a wonderful help or a damned nuisance working the sheep. He would spend his leisure time while Ann was away romping with the pet lamb who was in fact a fully-grown sheep. They would take turns to see who could knock whom over.

Broken leg number three came when he ran under our road-grader. He had his spine crushed as well. The kind thing to do would have been to put him down. But with a child in Adelaide threatening to run away from school if anything happened to Bob, and the fact that he was such a battler, we decided to nurse him through.

Complete with mattress, pillow and sleeping-bag, and all the tender, loving care in the world, Bob was kept as comfortable as possible. He had to be turned regularly and his limbs moved about to help circulation. Some days, he was very miserable

104

and howled a lot. Eventually he showed signs of wanting to drag himself around.

A local doctor agreed to X-ray Bob and discovered about four inches of bone missing in his spine. He offered to place a steel plate in Bob's hip and pin the spine, but at the time, it just seemed too expensive.

As time passed, Bob could be helped to sit up. Through all this he was always happy and seemed to understand whatever we said.

It became an ordeal to milk the cow. I had to wheel Bob in the wheelbarrow down to the cowyard, milk, carry the milk home and return to wheel Bob home again. I had to do this because Bob, in an attempt to come with me, would drag his hindquarters along the ground. This would wear sores on his legs.

On wash days, he lay on his mattress near the clothes line. When I worked in the garden, he had to be right next to me.

One day, as I was busily weeding, Bob dragged his foam mattress near to me. He shuffled around on it, seemingly unable to find the right spot. Jokingly, I said, 'Well, if you're not comfortable, go and get your pillow.'

He looked at me for a while, then dragged himself off to where the pillow was, brought it back and lay down again.

He shuffled and whimpered for some time, reminding me for the hundredth time that it would have been kinder to put him out of his misery.

'Well, if you're still not comfortable, you'd better go and get your rug,' I said.

So he once again dragged himself off and returned with the sleeping bag. With misty eyes, I made him as warm and comfortable as possible. He slept there in the warm sun for some time.

Bob eventually amazed us by starting to walk again—not on four legs, but on his two front legs. His terribly withered hindquarters were held in the air, just as if someone were holding them up as in a wheelbarrow race. This enabled him to get wherever he wanted to go and eventually he could put one hind leg on the ground and hop along a bit.

When he tired, he alternated between two and three legs.

Many people came to see him 'walking'. We wish we had taken a movie of him.

Bob's end came on a hot day when he attempted to get involved in some sheep work. Although we searched well into the night, he couldn't be found. Being a cripple, it turned out he had had to take the long way round. In the heat, he had perished although he was only about 100 yards from a water trough at home. We didn't find him for some time.

HOUDINI HOUND

Wendy Treloar, Cummins

Oscar was a bitser. No other description could possibly fit his pedigree. Now that he is dead, we can reflect on his past glories. Oscar had no particular tricks, pranks, or begging-on-his-hind-leg stories . . . his was just a lifelong saga of staying alive.

As a young puppy, he was friend to all the Fitzgerald children. For some time, Oscar seemed content to bask in the spoiling, but one day, he was put into the back of a farm utility and driven around the paddocks to check the sheep. From that day onwards, he was free!

He discovered he could jump up without the driver's knowing. Thus he escaped the indignity of being dressed up in doll's clothes, or being pushed around in an old wicker pram. He leapt aboard at every opportunity and with the wind whistling past his ears he sniffed the smell of sheep, female dogs on nearby farms, emus, kangaroos and rabbits.

The Brooker farm was some twenty miles from the Fitzgerald homestead and on one visit, Oscar was accidentally left behind.

He waited until sundown, then he set off. He sniffed all the tracks until he found the correct road and arrived home weary and footsore, but triumphant. He gave the worried family his most withering look and flounced out to his kennel.

From then on, Oscar roamed.

He scouted in the large nearby creeks and one winter was washed away under the bridge and downstream in a flash flood, twisting and bumping into the huge logs. Waterlogged, he eventually made it to the bank and, caked in mud, lay there, exhausted. The hard, setting clay saved his life. When he was examined by the vet, having managed to struggle home days after the searching was over, it was found his neck had been broken. It took weeks to get rid of the clay.

Recovery brought more adventures. He chased a fox into its hole. A terrible thumping was heard, and clouds of dust escaped from the hole. Out came the fox, but no Oscar. Spike Fitzgerald waited and whistled and dug deep into the lair. Poor Oscar. Surely he would be dead. Spike returned later in the day with a shovel to dig out the dog, but there he was, trotting home across the paddock, limping, ears drooping, bloodied and torn—but alive.

A passing kangaroo was an instant invitation to fight, especially as Oscar could leap sideways in the air like a fighting cock. It always confused the roos. Oscar would leap from his box on the motorbike as he went past.

At night rabbits, too, blinded by the spotlight, were good fun for Oscar. Oscar could leap and pounce simultaneously.

On his more manly excursions, he wandered one night across the road to Uncle Bas Fitzgerald's place. Not wanting his dog's pedigree to be mingled with Oscar's, Uncle Bas fired off the gun. Oscar was shot through his socks, ears and tail.

After his recovery, the kids dressed Oscar up and put earrings through the bullet holes in his ears.

Oscar accumulated all sorts of mates, and after one hot day's excursion, he and a friend took refuge in the shearing shed where some watered-down Lucijet was left. Oscar's mate slaked his thirst on the watered-down mixture, but Oscar drank his neat. His mate keeled over and died, but Oscar licked his lips and looked around for more.

Leaping into the farm truck during harvest involved a

different form of risk. Only Oscar survived the slipping forwards of a bulk bin. It squashed his mate.

The truck backed over him, but the sandy soil under the tyres caused him to be only a bit squashed. After a rubdown, Oscar staggered to his feet once more.

Eventually Oscar's escapades took their toll and he retired to his kennel daring, with a toothless growl, anyone to come near his territory.

The battered old dog's life ended but the kennel is still underneath the pine trees.

ALL FOUR BACK ON THE GROUND

Syd Nosworthy, Lucindale

When John Corbett arrived home with two border collie pups, he bedded them down in their kennels under restraint. The pups soon voiced their resentment of this treatment and as the sounds penetrated the kitchen, Mary, John's wife, remarked: 'It sounds as though we're in for some country music—a Slim Dusty concert.' Unwittingly, she had christened the pups.

Slim grew to be a tall, rather rangy dog. Dignified and aloof, he gave unswerving devotion to John, but treated with the utmost disdain approaches from anyone else.

Dusty was a complete contrast. Affable and gregarious, he soon learnt how to cajole the tastiest household morsels from Mary and developed a rotund figure not conducive to the rigours of a working life. He would obligingly work for anyone, but at a very leisurely pace. He was adept at backing round a building or any reasonable cover to keep out of John's view, but as the tail of the mob approached the gate, he would appear to hunt the last few sheep in and stand by for any plaudits that might be forthcoming. John was well aware of Dusty's habits but happily tolerated the friendly rogue.

'My dogs,' John always declared, 'are willing. Slim's willing to work and Dusty is willing to let him.'

A brush with a motor vehicle injured the youthful Slim and thereafter he carried one hind leg. It detracted little from his capacity for work and his speed around the paddocks invariably left Dusty floundering in his wake, floundering, but happily unconcerned.

One shearing season, however, Slim was again exercising his propensity for chasing motor vehicles. His collar caught in the wheel stud of a passing truck and he was whirled once around with the wheel and smashed heavily on to the bitumen surface. John, helped by the distraught truck driver, carried the unconscious dog to a makeshift shelter. Outwardly, there were no obvious injuries, but it was quite evident he had suffered serious injury—so evident that some observers suggested John should 'end his misery'.

By next day, Slim was conscious, but incapable of movement. He gave no response to John's presence and appeared quite oblivious of the milk and tasty morsels thrust beneath his nose. Dusty proceeded to give the performance of his life. He sat beside Slim and his soft whining and rapt attention not only told his concern, but he was obviously exhorting his friend to respond. He did respond, if only by a slight flicker of an eyelid.

Finally Dusty's pragmatic streak surfaced. He gobbled up the food, clearly thinking, 'There's no point in wasting it'.

Another factor was involved in Slim's eventual recovery. It was Julia Corbett, who had been a toddler when the pups arrived at the farm. They grew together. From the outset, Dusty and Julia were soul mates. Rolling and romping joyously on the lawn, their pleasure in each other's company was clear.

Slim watched these antics from close by though at first tending to shrink away from Julia's advances. But he did unbend, and she was the only person in his life to whom he did unbend.

Mary wasn't prepared for Slim's reaction one day when she reprimanded Julia and the child cried out in indignation. A menacing snarl from Slim gave a clear message of his views.

The day after Slim's accident, Julia came home from school and rushed to look at and comfort her friend. An infinitely feeble movement of his head and an even more feeble twitch of his tail proved that Slim was aware of her. Although he ignored the saucer of milk she proffered, he did attempt to swallow when she dipped her small hand in the milk and pushed it into his mouth, letting the drops fall on his tongue.

This ritual was repeated over and again throughout the weekend until he was swallowing milk squeezed from a sponge onto his tongue. Although Dusty kept up his daily performance, ending as usual with his determination to maintain his own strength, he was excited and delighted when Slim did raise his head and lap the milk from the saucer.

It took Slim about three weeks to recover sufficiently to struggle into a half-crouching position and ultimately to sit up and eat the food and drink on offer. During most of that time, he lay almost inert, but when Julia sat beside him gently stroking his head, his eyes and tail marked his appreciation.

It was a moment of jubilation when Slim finally struggled to his feet and after a few tentative, staggering steps began to walk with greater surety.

'Dad!' called an ecstatic Julia. 'Look, he's got all his feet on the ground!'

No-one ever knew what anatomical miracle had occurred for Slim but for the rest of his days he was back on four feet and never again carried that hind leg.

PART 7

KNOCK-OFF TIME

And when it's time to go, some are still hard at it while a few 'lucky' ones might get to retire. One thing's for sure, it's more a beginning than an end— they live on through their offspring

JUST A GENETIC HICCUP

Mike Hayes

Not all that long ago, when I went out to seek a replacement for Wally the Wonder Dog, I (naturally) got into quite deep conversation with the owner of the particular pup we eventually roped in to our Rural Empire.

'Y'know,' he reminisced, 'there was a bloke round Starpost way who never let a young dog have a go with his sheep until it'd spent at least a year as a rabbiter. I've noticed meself that if a dog's been a rabbit dog, he usually does all right out in the paddock.'

Purists might disagree, claiming a dog who has a taste for bunnying could easily be distracted while working if a rabbit happened to cross his path in mid-muster. I really don't know. Wal was a hopeless rabbiter. Once, when confronted by a ravening baby rabbit, he sat there shivering and whining and his sheep work was almost acceptable. But that bloke's opinion reminded me there are working dogs other than the sheep and cattle variety in the bush. The honest rabbit dog seems to have gone out of vogue these days, but back in pre-myxo times, we often had more of them about the place than sheepdogs.

I'm also about to break the rule about never giving dogs human characteristics. Anyone who's worked with one knows a dog's talents are entirely canine and it's unfair to treat them like people. However, how many of us have also thought to ourselves, 'I wonder what the little brown bugger's thinking?'

Old Sandy stirred on the cushion and half-heartedly attempted to reposition his rear end without awakening fully. The briquette fire was really pumping out the heat and Sandy's bum was getting uncomfortably hot. It felt a little like the old days, when he'd pick a nice shady spot to doze in the morning and, inadvertently having slept away three-quarters of the day, would wake to find the sun had shifted in the sky and he was quietly broiling himself.

112

Sandy chuckled in his sleep. Mrs Porter, who'd been diligently knitting an Essendon football club beanie for one of Nelda's boys, reached down and touched him gently.

'Shhhh!' she crooned softly. 'You're having a nightmare.'

'Nightmare be buggered!' thought Sandy to himself. The nightmares had gone long ago, coinciding with the time he'd been turned over to Mrs Porter and endured the long petrol-fumy trip from the bush where he'd been born, to the geriatric comfort of leafy Caulfield. The nightmares had always been part of the old days, along with the freedom and the thrill of the hunt . . . and the kids.

Sandy half rolled further away from the heater and, thankfully a bit cooler, drifted off in his mind back to those old days.

Sandy hadn't started life as a kids' dog. He'd been born, rather unexpectedly one quiet October morning, under 'Crackers' Hunt's woolshed.

Sandy's Mum was a grizzled old fox terrier bitch—not the dwarf, yappy ones you seem to get everywhere these days, but a stocky, medium-sized black and white dog called Annie. She may well not have been 100% foxie at all, but round those parts of western Victoria, that's the breed she was known as. Hunt half-heartedly tolerated her as a relatively long-serving member of his huge pack of rabbit dogs. Like most of the mutts, she was allowed free range of the bare, dusty acres of Hunt's front paddocks. Only the savage ones, the Alsations and boxers, were tied up, and then only since the Shire sent Crackers a threatening letter after old Jim Polkinghorn's horse was spooked by a few marauding dogs on its painful way up to the Bluffs where Jim spent his time laying rabbit and wild dog traps.

Hunt hadn't earned his nickname without reason. Periodically, usually after a demented drinking bout, when the locals referred to him as 'moonstruck', he'd randomly select a few members of his canine rabble, tie them up by their hind legs to the low limb of the sheep-killing tree, and shoot them.

Later, in a fit of remorse, he'd drive all the way into Melbourne, select a few unwanted strays from the Animal Hospital and return with them to keep his pack numbers up.

113

Crackers fed the dogs better than he fed himself. Every time he slaughtered a killer, he'd wrap only a handful of chops and bung them into the icebox for himself. The rest he'd diligently boil up, to kill any hydatid tapeworms, and distribute to his hordes.

His initial reaction to the Shire's letter had 'moonstruck' him too. After tying up the malefactors, he selected a few innocents from the other bony hounds around the place and summarily executed them.

Sandy's puppyhood had been filled with memories of Hunt's little quirks. That's when the nightmares started. The frightening thuds of his shotgun and the unmistakeable smell of blood in the dust engraved themselves on his consciousness at a very early age. At night, or during his exhausted puppy-dozes during the day, he'd mentally act out the one thing he feared most—seeing Hunt's dusty boots making their way to wherever he dreamed he was hiding, watching the big gnarled hand reaching into his hiding-place, hearing the click of the long, glinting stick he carried . . . waiting for the thump.

Not that Crackers was particularly brutal to Annie and her litter. He seemed to be especially intrigued by the pups. Quite often, he'd stop whatever he was doing when he worked in the yards or the shed and come over to inspect the wriggling, round bundles of new life. He'd cup them in his hands, run nicotine-yellowed fingers along their backs and hold them up to his face, examining them closely.

Sandy never found out why Hunt was so interested in him and the others. He never got to leave the property. He never heard the pub talk down at the Criterion in town, eleven miles away from Hunt's rundown selection.

'They reckon Crackers Hunt's got a litter of dingoes out of one of his mongrel bitches.'

'Yair. Jim Polkinghorn reckons an old warrigal musta snuck down out of the Bluffs one night and slipped her one.'

'Fair dinkum? Crackers don't wanna let the wildlife people hear about that.'

'No. Or some of his neighbours. Those big old wool cockies up past Ringworm Springs'd be onto him like a shot.'

'A shot? More like a whole lot of flamin' shots.'

Sandy heard none of that. He just sucked nourishment from

114

his mother's dugs, wrestled with his siblings and made sure he was deep under the woolshed whenever he sensed that Hunt was on one of his rampages.

Eventually, Hunt's secret did reach unwelcome ears. One morning a government car lurched into the yard. Two men in suits spoke briefly to Hunt and they all came over to where Annie was feeding her litter under the woolshed water tank. Sandy sensed the animosity of the two oddly-dressed strangers. He also sensed the aura of fury that was starting to emanate from Crackers. Sandy knew. Soon there would be loud thumps—and the smell of blood in the dust.

Quietly, he backed away from his mum's belly and slid into the darkness under the shed. The other pups sucked on. There were the thumps. The strangers loaded four small, still bodies into a sugar bag and threw it into the boot of their car. Crackers stewed for the rest of the afternoon, then finally went into the house for his shotgun. More thumps. More blood and dust. After sundown, when Sandy finally emerged from his hiding place, he found Annie missing. He went hungry that night, and next morning. Late in the day, Hunt found him curled up under the tank. The madness in him having gone, the cocky picked up the little tan-coloured pup and spoke surprisingly softly to him.

'You poor little bastard,' he muttered. 'You poor, unwanted little bastard.'

When Crackers turned the pup over to us, Sandy was about a year old. Hunt made no secret of his ancestry.

'An old black 'n' white foxie I once had, got herself knocked off by one of Jim Polkinghorn's dingoes—probably when we were sawin' logs up at the Bluffs,' he explained. 'He'll be a good rabbit dog and you won't have to worry about him and sheep. He's too small to get into any of that sort of caper.'

Crackers' uncharacteristic generosity had been prompted by a chance meeting we'd had with another member of his motley crew of canines. Half a dozen of us had gone off after school to dig out rabbit burrows. In those days, before myxo decimated the rabbit population around our way, we discovered that rabbits proved a useful way of relieving the poverty so many

115

valley people lived in. Our inventive mother found out we could get 2/6 a pair for them from a chiller operator who toured the district buying bunnies for the markets in Melbourne. In summer, especially, we were able to hurry home from school, grab an old mattock and a couple of shovels and earn what seemed to us a veritable fortune by doing the rounds of the thousands of massive rabbit warrens in the volcanic country up behind the village. Our modus operandi was simple. We'd watch where the rabbits ran when we disturbed them as we approached their warrens, then set to digging them out. In the soft soil, it was an easy matter to follow the tunnels and just before the end, reach in, grab the residents and despatch them quickly with a twist of the neck.

It would have been a lot easier with a good rabbit dog, but we got by. For a short time, we experimented with ferrets, but found they invariably ate any victims they found in the burrows, then curled up and went to sleep. Sometimes we'd be able to dig them out wasting valuable rabbiting time but often they'd get so far into the bowels of the warrens that it'd be impossible to find them. The only thing we could do then, to avoid getting into strife for arriving home after dark, was elect one of our number to sit up—sometimes half the night—beside the burrow, waiting for the ferrets to wake and report back for duty. No, dogs would have been far more useful than ferrets but, seeing we were making do on our own, we never actually got round to looking for one—until we fell in with Crackers.

On this particular afternoon, we were heading down from the Bluffs with twenty or so dead rabbits hanging head down from our Scout belts when Bruce suddenly called out: 'Hey! There's a dog stuck in the dam.' The dam in question was a water supply reservoir for the village. It had concrete sides and we knew from past experience how difficult it was for man or beast to scramble back up the smooth slope if they ventured into the water. The dam was heavily Cyclone-fenced to ensure no mishaps occurred, but it seemed that this time the dog—a large black, white and brindle pointer—had found a way through.

When we scrambled down, climbed the fence and investigated further, we could see he'd been there a while. His claws were worn away and his feet bleeding from trying to drag his way out of the reservoir. The poor old dog was knackered. He wouldn't have lasted another five minutes. Bruce slid the rabbits off his belt and we joined it to ours to fashion a lifeline with which we could lower him down the concrete slope towards the rapidly tiring dog. He managed to get a good grip of the long floppy ears and we soon had the dog safely grassed.

It took a couple of phone calls to work out who owned the pointer, who happened to be named Mackie. Crackers Hunt claimed the dog and asked if we could take him over to his place. He couldn't pick him up himself because he didn't have a car and was too busy lamb-marking to spare the time to walk.

We returned Mackie to his owner (quaking a little inside because we'd all heard the stories about Hunt's craziness) but instead of going berserk, as we'd been warned he might, Crackers went over to the shed and came back with Sandy.

'You little buggers'd probably find a good use for this little tyke,' he growled. 'He's no good to me and it'd probably do us both a favour if you give him a home.' That's when he explained Sandy's pedigree. We unquestioningly accepted his assurances about the unlikelihood of the little dog worrying sheep. After all, wasn't he all we'd ever needed? At last we'd got a dog. Our rabbiting enterprise would now be able to move into top gear.

About six weeks later, old Jim Polkinghorn brought the news to the village that he'd driven by Crackers Hunt's place and noticed all the dogs seemed to be dead. The gossip really started flying when the police from town went to investigate and found Hunt had indeed taken his shotgun to the lot—including poor old Mackie. He'd saved the last cartridge for himself. I remember the adults talking late at night about Crackers having had a wife who'd moved out of the district years before.

'That's when they say it all started. He wasn't a bad sort of bloke before then.' But by then us kids weren't all that interested any more and had forgotten most of the gory details—and so, I suppose, had Sandy.

The little dog's nightmares did indeed stop when he moved in with the kids. The small, light tan pup with pricked ears and white-tipped, cocked tail discovered an idyllic world, far removed from tank stands, shearing sheds and nightmarish thumps. He was allowed to sleep on an old blanket on the wide verandah which fronted our cottage. There were no terrifying sounds or frightening smells. There were always at least two feeds of rabbit and bones a day. In winter he was even allowed in to doze by the open fire before everyone went to bed. But, best of all, there were the afternoon excursions Up The Back to hunt rabbits.

He'd dabbled in the sport a few times in the last few months. Hunt's lack of control over his dogs meant Sandy and a few older dogs had been free to explore the back paddocks, relishing the tantalising smells along the sheep paths and wallaby tracks and occasionally thundering helter-skelter, with hysterical barks, if a rabbit happened to spook in front of them. But it hadn't been nearly as exciting as rabbiting with the kids. Sandy had no terminology to express it but, really, he'd found Heaven on Earth up there on the flat-topped volcanic bluffs behind the village, where the wind rattled through the uplifted arms of the dead trees, ringbarked fifty years earlier by the first selectors, and where the tussocks grew over exciting tunnels down which a keen young rabbit dog found limitless adventure.

The kids had originally only wanted a dog that would spook rabbits from out of their squats in the tussocks and drive them in panic to the warrens, from where they could be excavated. But for Sandy, that was never enough. The dingo side of him would allow him to leap forward from a standing start like an arrow. In a few short, frantic yards, he'd grab a fleeing rabbit by the scruff of its neck. A quick shake and the bunny'd be history.

The fox terrier genes in Sandy had a hunting edge to them, too, but they also saw to it that he insisted on taking over the actual digging-out of the warrens. In true foxy style, Sandy would scrabble frantically through the soft earth until he could snap up the quivering rabbit at the end of the tunnel. In larger warrens he was even able to wriggle down the burrows and drag their occupants out one at a time. Unlike the ill-fated ferrets, he never snacked or went to sleep on the job. Over the years he developed one or two proud scars from where we'd accidentally nicked him with the mattock or the edge of the shovel when he got in our way, so keen was he to better our efforts at digging out the warrens.

Then there were the foxes. With their scalps fetching seven and six a pop at the police station in town, Sandy opened a whole new world of wealth to us. He occasionally kept them pinned in the warrens where he'd chased them, but mostly he'd run them down and subdue them in a welter of raised hackles, bared teeth, splashing saliva and frightening savagery. Invariably in a head-on confrontation, one of the kids would have to drag a slavering Sandy away from his quarry in order to recover enough of the fox to prove it did, indeed, once possess a scalp.

At three years of age, Sandy's mixed breeding didn't appear to be in any doubt. Sure, he was small—about half the size of a normal warrigal—but his build, his colouring and his jaunty tail bore no resemblance to any fox terrier anyone in the district had ever seen. And there was something else about Sandy that suggested that quite a bit of the domestic dog in him had been suppressed. He'd never look a human straight in the eye. He never played with the kids. Whereas in his puppy days, he'd bounce around with us with humour and enthusiasm, he now embarked on his daily hunting trips with a lope and a look of guilt about him. It was obviously not just fun anymore. Deep within him a small voice was telling him that hunting was fair dinkum—something a true professional never just fooled around with.

Looking back now, it was also fair to say that Sandy was never a particularly obedient dog. He never really responded to a command. To get him to stop doing something, we'd just about have to drag him away physically. If we wanted him to follow us, we'd have to move off first, hinting that perhaps there was something better along the track. He never responded to whistles. He did what he damn well liked. The kids didn't really notice it, I suppose because in those days, what we wanted and what Sandy wanted were pretty much along the same lines anyway. The perpetually guilty look was perhaps the strangest feature of the little dog. Apart from never really obeying us, he'd never really done anything to feel guilty about—not then.

The crackling, brown days of summer passed slowly. During

119

the Christmas school holidays we usually went Up The Back later in the day, when it wasn't so bakingly hot. Sandy slept under the house where it was beautifully cool. They were deep sleeps, completely free of the nightmares that had disturbed his rest as a pup.

That particular holiday break, a new influence entered Sandy's life. Lady was an eighteen-month-old rabbit dog—mostly fox terrier—not unlike what we imagined Sandy's Mum, the ill-fated Annie, would have been like. Sandy accepted her inclusion in our hunting ranks without rancour. He even allowed her to take over his spot on the verandah, although by then he actually preferred the hiding place provided by his comfortable little depression in the dust under the house. And out across the hills, Lady proved an efficient partner to the little dingo cross. When they flushed out rabbits and foxes, they worked as a team, herding them towards the appropriate warrens where the two of them took half the time to dig out their quarry.

With the extra money we earned from our rabbiting, we were able to transform the drab paddock at the front of the cottage with exotic garden plants, imported all the way from Melbourne. We even extended our formerly desperate water supply—complete with a fish pond—and built a bush-pole pergola which helped make a sad mockery of the other dusty front yards in the village.

The vegetable seeds we sent away for produced proud ranks of tomatoes and rambling pumpkin vines, welcome additions to a monotonous diet of mutton, rabbit or yabbie in those days when a camp pie, lettuce, grated processed cheese and half a tomato were considred a gourmet salad, and the blatantly American hot dog was prosaically referred to as a 'sav and roll'. Sandy and Lady's contribution to our improved quality of life was greatly appreciated, even by the smaller kids.

And so were their pups when they arrived. Our Mum allowed Lady one litter before sending her to the vet in town to be 'fixed up'. There were three in the litter—two nondescript bitches, which we managed to palm off on other families interested in emulating our rabbiting successes, and a strapping chocolate and white lad we named Pongo.

Pongo seemed to have inherited none of his father's characteristics. He was large for a fox terrier—even the mongrel strains we accepted as pedigree—and he looked nothing like a dingo. Our family group became the top rabbiting team in the valley. Where Sandy on his own had been impressive and Sandy and Lady had been perfection, Sandy, Lady and Pongo were the ultimate.

We couldn't really claim to have had a hand in it, despite the quality of our hunting team, but about the time Pongo was coming into his own, rabbit numbers started to fall off. It was all due to the myxo plague doing its grisly job with silent efficiency. Uneatable sick and blind rabbits, oozing pus from their eyes and nostrils, started to outnumber the healthy ones we once sent away to market. The chiller stopped calling. The easy money dried up. No-one wanted to risk serving up one of those pathetic, emaciated creatures for Sunday lunch.

Lady and Pongo settled down to a less vigorous existence— happily accepting a greater emphasis on just being kids' pets. We still went on regular rambles Up The Back and often returned with the odd fox or two, but life was becoming less feral for us. Besides, the older kids were starting to go to high school in town and didn't get back home during the week in time to fit in much outdoor activity. Sandy suddenly found himself with time on his paws.

At first he took out his newly developed frustrations and resulting bad temper on Pongo. On the occasional afternoon we elected to go bush, a dam of emotion and instinct would burst somewhere within the little dog's psyche. Out there in his element, it'd sometimes prove too much and often he'd break away from the chase, or even from a battle with a fox, and turn savagely on his son.

The fights were terrifying. Pongo, although a gentler soul than his old man, was much bigger and, if not in the same league in terms of savagery, at least wasn't going to be one to stand by and be done over. He knew about self-preservation. Sandy, with his inbred savagery, never gave quarter. We'd drag them apart, take them home separately on leashes and keep them away from each other for a week while they sulked, their mouths swollen from the taste of their shared blood.

About then, the complaints about sheep-killing started coming in.

Sandy drank deeply from the four-gallon drum under the downpipe. The taste in his mouth stirred uncomfortable memories. It reminded him of loud noises, strange stillnesses and that frightening smell mingled with dust. Today's trip Up The Back hadn't been much better than the last. Although he wouldn't admit it to any other dog, Pongo seemed to be starting to get the better of him. Perhaps it was because he was larger—and younger.

Sandy had originally planned to go straight back under the house and try to sleep off the pain and discomfort of his newest wounds. But for the moment he just savoured the water in his belly and sniffed the still night air. It was warm and dark. From above the village, along the flats before the ground started to rise upwards to the Bluffs, he could hear the sheep calling to each other. Their bleating was full of the insecurity and half-panic which always tinged their conversation. It was strange that he'd only just started to notice them.

Back in the only half-remembered days at Crackers Hunt's, he'd grown accustomed to their greasy smell, tinged with that same aroma of fear they always exuded. You could hardly miss it when you lived under the shearing shed. Whenever Crackers brought his sheep in, the smell permeated the whole universe, the fear component getting even stronger as he put them through the confusion and, sometimes, agony of the sheepyards.

In Sandy's adolescent hunting years, the sheep and their smell had still been there. The dusty grey forms fleeing in terror ahead of the dogs and the kids as they crossed the paddocks on their way Up The Back had provided momentary distraction, but nothing more. He'd never needed to pay much attention to them. In those days, the rabbit and fox hunting had been everything.

Occasionally they'd come across a dead one Up The Back. The smell then had been far more interesting. First there was the heady stench of decay and something had replaced the fear—something far more satisfying and more in keeping with the feelings that flooded his being after a day's rabbiting. But these days, Sandy found himself paying more and more attention to them. There was an air about them that even quelled much of the occasional anger which caused him to

122

vent his confused wrath on Pongo. Yes, sheep definitely required closer scrutiny.

The last light went out in the cottage. Barely noticing Lady's exhausted snore from the corner of the verandah, Sandy slid quietly past and sneaked quickly down the track towards the Marsdens' place. He didn't know why, but somehow he knew what he planned to do wouldn't sit well with the humans asleep in the cottage. He'd always had the feeling that they disapproved of him. As he'd grown older he'd found it more and more difficult to feel at ease in their presence.

He slid under the chicken wire and almost ran slap bang into Darkie. Darkie was the Marsdens' kelpie. Sandy hadn't had a lot to do with him until recently, when they'd met during a Progress Association meeting outside the village hall. They'd both observed protocol by weeing on a clump of tussock and boldly scratching the dust over it with their hind paws. Then they'd circled each other, with just the right amount of hackle-raising before sniffing suspiciously at each other's rears. Darkie's scent explained to Sandy that the kelpie wasn't a bad sort of bloke after all. He was never really keen on stacking on a blue and was more than happy to comply with any suggestion that they go for a bit of a wander up around the hills.

While the humans had continued to snarl at each other inside the hall, the two dogs poked leisurely around the community precincts, emptying their bladders on various landmarks, sharing a whole variety of fascinating smells and generally relishing each other's company. They even terrorised Warren's chooks for a while and studied a distant mob of sheep through the ringlock fence at the back of the houses. It could have gone further, but a shrill whistle from down near the hall turned Darkie's head and, obeying another instinct totally alien to Sandy, he trotted compliantly back to his boss's ute. Sandy followed him down more out of loyalty to his new mate than anything else.

But that had been in the early days of their relationship. Tonight, like on other recent nights, they had a whole program planned. Together they breached the barrier of the ringlock fence, Darkie sailing over and Sandy wriggling under a loose bottom strand. Darkie took the lead. He knew his way around the paddocks, although not generally in the dead of night. He cast wide to where he knew the sheep were camped. This late there was no bleating from the mob. Sandy could smell their peace of mind. It didn't last long. Darkie had reached the apex of his cast. They weren't Marsden's sheep, so the mob didn't know him personally. But they knew his kind. To humans, kelpies and other sheepdogs were merely animals with an instinct to work. To sheep and other animals, something within their scent and presence gave off the clear warning that they, like all canines, were just another predator.

The mob shifted to its feet and started warily back towards where Sandy crouched. They maintained a fair amount of order, not yet completely dominated by panic. They sensed rather than saw Darkie moving back and forth in the darkness where they'd been dozing. They didn't realise Sandy was there in the tussocks until, about the same time, he saw their leaders in the gloom.

Darkie had them well held. He used their reticence about venturing any further in Sandy's direction to guide them quietly to the eastern corner of the paddock where he jammed them conveniently into the V formed by the two fence lines. Darkie dropped back to press the stragglers in. Unable to progress in any direction, the sheep stood motionless and confused, still not really aware of their plight. Sandy was ready.

He came like an arrow, his ears flattened against his head for speed, and plunged into the forest of legs, which started shuffling and stamping with the first realisation of terror. A young ewe, about a year old, just a two-tooth, put her head down and Sandy took her on the cheek. The suddenness and speed of his strike pulled her down. The sheep were all small-framed Merinos and Sandy's lack of stature suddenly wasn't a drawback, especially considering the ferocity of his attack.

Behind him, Darkie barked a couple of times, excited by the sudden aroma of blood. But the excitement wasn't strong enough yet to override his basic instinct to hold the sheep. The killer in his genes lay further below the surface than with Sandy.

Around the growling dog and the wildly kicking ewe, the mob spilt. Sheep jumped over Sandy's back as he relinquished hold of her cheek and burrowed desperately into the inconvenient woolly wrinkles protecting her throat. A bigger ewe would have shaken him off by now. Suddenly, Darkie blundered through the sheep, allowing them to escape. Slightly ashamed of what he saw as his dereliction of duty, he leaped about behind Sandy, panting and woofing noisily in the confusion and dark. Below Sandy's front paws, the ewe suddenly stopped struggling. Darkie was now beside him, inhibitions gone, slurping thirstily at the dark fluid gushing around them. Sandy growled the traditional warning: 'Piss off. I'm here first.'

Darkie, a little hurt but mindful of protocol, dropped away and went around to the rear end of the ewe, where she'd voided her bladder and bowels in terror. He worried at the soft area in front of her udder. Sandy moved his attention to the ewe's flank, burrowing through her soft insides in search of a morsel of liver or kidney. They both sensed the intruders at the same time.

To Darkie, the smells and sounds were familiar. The bright light that momentarily blinded him was very similar to the two on the boss's ute, and the stronger one he carried on the front seat to shine out fox eyes before sounding the gun at them. In fact, the smells coming from beyond the light grew even more familiar. There was the boss . . . and another like him.

'Fucking hell. It *is* bloody Darkie!'

To Sandy, the smells and noises were to be interpreted differently. Sure, there was the aroma of man. And although the light wasn't exactly shining directly in his eyes, he knew it to be a human force. But distinct among all the smells and sounds was the oily menace of the guns they carried and the distinctive click of them being straightened. They were smells and sounds from his puppy days. Soon there would be those heavy thuds—and that smell, not unlike the strong scent arising in invisible waves from around the dead ewe.

Sandy stayed on his belly and slid backwards into the tussocks, keeping low and quiet until the sudden brightness thrown from the spotlight had passed. He wondered at the way Darkie stood bolt upright with his tail wagging and his tongue lolling stupidly, gullibly waiting for the humans to reach him. Then Sandy started silently back towards the village. As he strained back under the bottom wire of the fence, he heard the single thud behind him.

The cockies in the valley held several meetings to discuss the sheep-killings. The first one was called more than a week after Bill Marsden sadly accepted the task of destroying Darkie.

'The best bloody dog I'll ever have,' he commented later.

But Darkie's demise hadn't ended the killings and maulings. Two nights later, in the very same paddock, another three ewes were killed. Two had been lightly snacked, but the third seemed to have been slaughtered and left. Us kids didn't get to go inside to the meetings. Our parents went and we could hear the angry shouts from inside the hall while we clambered over the playground equipment.

'I'm losing my best bloody studs. I paid nearly a pound for most of 'em.'

'Well, it's not my dogs that are killing them. They're tied up all the time whenever they're not workin'.'

Notices appeared in the local rag, the *Express*: 'Let it be known that any dogs found wandering on Rocky Hill will be destroyed. Signed , Clem Manly,' and 'Poison baits have been laid at Wattle Glenn. Signed, Alf Darby.'

The threats stirred up dog owners and parents alike. A lusty debate about the dangers to young children followed the warning from Alf. For a while, Jim Polkinghorn enjoyed a boom time. However, despite his efforts, no dingoes or wild dogs were trapped on any of the afflicted properties and the sheep-killings continued. Saddened cockies begrudgingly put down their own dogs, just to keep the peace, admidst widespread accusations. And still the killings went on.

It took a while, but us kids started working out who was really to blame. We didn't twig at first when Sandy showed hardly any enthusiasm for jaunts Up The Back. The little mongrel was generally too knocked-up after his nocturnal jaunts to show much interest in daytime activity. He stayed under the house whenever we were around at weekends and holidays but sometimes, when we came back from school, we noticed Sandy wasn't around. If we decided to go up in the hills, Pongo and Lady would obligingly fall in behind us and we'd give Sandy up as a bad job. Then, up in the back country, way out of sight of the village, we'd suddenly find him loping guiltily through the tussocks, so preoccupied that sometimes he wouldn't notice us until we were almost upon him. The penny

126

started dropping when, on too many occasions, we'd find him dragging a hunk of fresh meat around, or sniffing a ripe carcass hidden behind a fallen tree. By then, Sandy had his secret caches well organised.

We really knew what was going on after a couple of occasions when, once we'd reached the all-surveying vantage point of the Bluffs, we'd see a mob of sheep spilling in terror across a distant paddock and maybe catch the merest glimpse of a fox-like form slicing through the middle of them like a small red shark. Fox-like, indeed. But foxes didn't hunt sheep like that.

When you're ten or eleven, it's hard to know what to do in a situation like that. True, old Sandy wasn't what you'd call a kids' pet. He'd grown far too secretive and feral for that. But he'd been with us a long time. He'd been part of our young lives for as long as most of us could remember. At that age we couldn't be noble like the cockies who'd been prepared to sacrifice their own dogs in their desperate attempt to find the sheep-killer. Someone had got *Dusty* out of the school library. Most of us had read it. We knew the rules. That fictional dog's life seemed a close parallel to Sandy's, but the big difference was that Sandy was our dog. If anyone expected us to dob him in—well they just didn't understand the bond that exists between kids and dogs, even grumpy little psychopaths like Sandy. The thought of him being found out terrified us. He'd been a mate for too long.

It seems amazing now that the oldies never twigged. I remember big, bluff, Alan Grey dropping round and guffawing in his honest, loud voice, 'If yer don't watch out, that little dingo-lookin' bloke of yours'll be out killing sheep like that other dawg.' Our hearts stood still that afternoon.

Sandy didn't kill sheep all the time. Like Crackers Hunt, he only seemed to be gripped by the madness occasionally. In winter, especially, he tended to stick fairly close to home. Then, with spring and lambing, he broke out again. This time our Mum sprung him with a half-chewed lamb. I don't know if she put two and two together at first. Maybe she just thought it was his first offence. However, it proved the first step in Sandy's undoing.

Mum could be a hard woman. The bush tends to do that

to people, but she had a soft spot for dogs. After telling us in hushed tones what she'd discovered Sandy doing, she ruled that he could no longer have a free rein. Sandy had to be tied up. It didn't last long. No dog enjoys being chained up and that genetic hiccup in Sandy made his plight even more pathetic. It wasn't just that the sudden loss of freedom took the fire out of his eyes. It was as if a life force had drained from that wiry little tan body. Even the cocky tail dropped in defeat.

'Sometimes I think it'd be better if we had him shot,' Mum'd say with increasing frequency. We quailed internally, but we knew she'd never have it done. Dog people are like that.

God knows where, or even why, she dug Mrs Porter up from, but one Sunday she arrived in a car carrying a special wicker basket to relieve us of our prisoner. She examined Sandy closely and said in that funny baby talk a lot of city people revert to when addressing dogs, 'Well, Sandy, are you going to come and keep little me company?'

Sandy went along quietly. He obviously wasn't exactly heartbroken at leaving our company. Like I said before, he was never particularly affectionate and probably thought we'd let him down pretty badly in the long run, anyway. It didn't really explain, though, why the almost-forgotten spring returned to his step as he pranced up into the back of the car, ignoring any suggestion that he use the wicker basket. Crikey, even the tail was back up at the top of the mast.

As the car growled away in a roll of dust, I experienced a feeling of relief that stays strong in my memory, even today. Maybe Sandy experienced the same thing. Anyway, there were never any more sheep-killings.

Before drifting off completely, Sandy recollected briefly how closed-in he'd first felt at Mrs Porter's. Oh, the accommodation and the catering were fair enough, but the dark house with its benign, apathetic smells and that tiny backyard ... But at least the nightmares stopped.

Oh yes, back there with the kids, after the confrontations with the sheep, they'd started again ... just like those of his puppy days, only even worse. The thumps, the still bodies, the smells ... only this time he knew they were coming for him.

It had been even worse when he was on the chain. Then he'd had little to do but sleep . . . and dream those terrifying, guilty dreams. That's why he hadn't worried about coming away with the old, sweet-smelling human. At least she wasn't a threat. Maybe she could take him away from the nightmares. And she had. They'd gone.

Old Sandy breathed a heavy sigh and Mrs Porter looked over her glasses at him again. 'Still having bad dreams?' she asked again quietly.

'No way,' thought Sandy to himself.

Outside, cars hissed through the drizzle. The radiation from the briquette heater was just right for an old retired hunting dog . . . even an old retired half-dingo. As he slept, his only dreams were pleasant golden ones, full of excited puppy yelps from young humans, and rabbits hurtling desperately through the sun-kissed tussocks.

GOOD ALL-ROUND

Wally Karger, Vale Park

This is a true story of the life of a pup. We lived on a farm in the Adelaide Hills, running about 200 sheep, three cows, seventy chooks and ten geese. We trained Lassie from a six-week-old pup. Obedience was important, so she learned to sit and come at once. She also learned to pick up small articles and to put them into our hands, or in a bucket, or on a chair, wherever we told her to put them. We always gave her a small crumb or cornflake as reward.

Before she was six months old, she was able to bring me a pair of pliers, a screwdriver or a box of matches. She could even bring them out to where we were working in the paddock. Later, she learned to bring some sheep shears so we could treat fly-struck sheep.

In 1955, a bushfire burnt us out and we were broke. Lassie had become a sheepdog which we could lend to our neighbours. Our own sheepyards had been destroyed in the fire.

I had to go to work off the farm and Lassie would lie with no interest in sheep until 6 o'clock on Saturday morning. Then she would be at the door and I'd just say 'fetch the sheep in' and after I had lit the fire and had breakfast, the sheep would be waiting at the gate to go into the neighbour's yards. She was both a yard dog and paddock dog and rarely left a sheep behind even in the rough hills or scrub.

She was good with the geese too. If they wandered, my wife just had to say, 'Lass, the geese are on the road'. Very slowly, the geese would then be driven back to the dam where Lassie would watch them for an hour, sometimes not even allowing them out of the water.

Our neighbour, Murray, had Dorset Horn cross sheep and we had black-faced Suffolk rams. Murray's lambs always seemed to crawl under the fence and would join up with our black-faced ones. We always tried to drive them out before they got boxed up.

One Sunday, Murray phoned and told us to watch Lassie who was over on the hill. There she was, very slowly, walking between fourteen big weaner lambs of Murray's and our mob. While the lambs were feeding , she worked them gently towards the fence. Then she put them through the hole and moved them up into Murray's yard where she lay and watched them with her head on her paws.

Lassie knew our three cows by name; and once introduced to visitors, could single them out and drop a ball at their feet if she was asked to.

One of her last chores, at the age of fourteen, was particularly memorable. We were irrigating from the River Murray. I had left my rubber boots down in the lucerne where the sprinklers were.

I was tired and weary, so I said, 'Fetch my rubber boots, Lass'. The poor old girl loped down to the lucerne, and after ten minutes appeared with one boot.

I repeated the order and she brought the other to the door. By this time, it was almost dark, but there were my boots.

The look she gave me almost said what I was thinking, 'My time is almost up.'

When I decided we must put her down, I went to find her. She was curled up in her kennel in our garage, already dead.

STIFF AS A BOARD

Bill Hewett, Balaklava

Jock was a wedding present—a ball of black and white fluff, with plum pudding spots on his nose.

With practically no training, except basic 'come', 'go', 'sit,' 'stay,' 'speak', he seemed to know exactly what was needed, and by the age of six months, was an almost perfect sheepdog. For nearly sixteen years he performed almost everything expected of him and he still enjoyed putting chooks back in their house when they escaped. But he developed some annoying habits.

As he got older and slower, he needed a spell and a drink more often. It didn't save any time giving him a bowl of water in the yards. He had his own pet trough 100 yards away and took his time going and coming.

Jock never slept in a house or shed or drum or kennel. Even in old age and in mid-winter, he would still sleep flat out on his side in the middle of the yard. It was not uncommon to go out on a frosty morning and find him snow-white, covered in frost, and as stiff as a board.

I would pick him up and prop him up against the silo on the sunny side.

He would slowly move around it, following the sun, until he had thawed out enough to walk away for a feed and drink and a look in the sheepyards to see if anything was happening.

One cold day he did not thaw out. We had lost the best friend and helper our family had ever had.

BUGGA-YA

Maxine Brown, Padthaway

Rick, our part-time workman, friend and farmhand, was always intrigued at the names Bob, the dog, answered to, particularly 'Bugga-ya'. So I wrote a poem in explanation. He was such a loyal, loving old dog and he really did think as one with my husband, Terry—so much so that when he was very deaf in later years, he still knew exactly what to do and did it well, without commands.

Of course, if the sheep did need to go into a different paddock from the one Bob thought, it took much waving of arms and carrying on to attract his attention and get the message across. This was a rather exhausting exercise and frustrating too.

When Terry was talking to stockmen, travellers etc., Bob would stand alongside them with his head just touching Terry's leg and with his head down, listening but not moving for ages— or as long as it took the discussion (sometimes hours!). Occasionally, when they laughed, he would look up and give a doggy laugh too and then go back to his listening.

He was a great yard dog and good in trucks. Once we unloaded a triple-decker semi of lambs from interstate. They were cold and slow, so Bob had a big job to move them. He forgot he was in a truck, and not the yards, and jumped clean over the side of the top deck. He was so very sore and sorry, but survived.

Bob's one fault was 'women', and when life got boring, he would take off. It's funny how a dog knows a bitch is on heat ten to twelve kilometres away. People got to know him and he managed to calm their fury and persuade them to feed him, or just give us a ring. Most times though, he would just turn up at home next morning.

I think people eventually realised how good a sheepdog he was because there seem to be lots of longish-haired, black sheepdogs about—much valued by their owners, and looking a lot like Bob.

Before he went deaf, he was shrewd enough on these conjugal errands to get off the road and hide in the grass when a vehicle approached.

He was eventually hit by a vehicle when he could no longer hear. There was some comfort knowing that he died having done what he enjoyed most.

We really miss old Bob. He really was like one of the family.

'BUGGA-YA'

The working dogs were Bob and Sal
The farmer's friend, his own best pal
But puzzled stockmen wondered how
They got the name of 'Bugga-ya'

Bob was priceless, loved to work
But hot days tempted him to shirk
A cool sheep trough a tempting lurk
And worth the threat of 'Bugga-ya'

Together they worked just as one
But in his haste to see it done
Bob would often 'beat the gun'
And answered then to 'Bugga-ya'

Now Rick came working to the farm
Admired the dogs with all their charm
But then he found to his alarm
This dog responds to 'Bugga-ya'

133

When travellers and stockmen leaned on the gate
Bob, in his wisdom, kept close to his mate
Listened intently, willing to wait
Never a whisper of 'Bugga-ya'

Bob grew old and could not hear
Still worked the sheep, his love most dear
Commands ignored though men were near
He couldn't hear that 'Bugga-ya'

But still his faithfulness excelled
He knew his boss's mind so well
It saved them having then to yell
And give commands of 'Bugga-ya'

But Bob was still a boy at heart
The lure of sex was strong in part
He visited his doggy tart
'Now where's that dog gone? "Bugga-ya" '

Six miles away we found him dead
A vehicle had hit his head
Happily we know he's bred
Lots of little 'Bugga-yas'

We miss our trusting faithful friend
His daughter now the sheep does tend
Our neighbours all his offspring send
To work their sheep with . . . 'Bugga-ya'

THE OLD DOG TAKES GLORY

Angela Goode

On our place there is a funny-looking black and tan kelpie called Roy. He's missing a few teeth and his bark is a bit hoarse, because, at ten, he is a fairly senior fellow.

Now whether it's because he has just become a father of nine to the bitch down the road, or he's suffering dementia, Roy has suddenly started backing sheep, that trick of jumping onto their backs to push them tightly together in a yard or race. He has never shown the slightest tendency to such extravagances, being instead the type of dog that silently stalks the sheep with his rump in the air and his elbows and head low to the ground, hypnotising them with his rather bulbous eyes.

So it was with great excitement that we all ran up to the shearing shed during crutching a fortnight ago to witness this great event. The boss was fairly glowing with pride. 'I don't know what's got into the old fool,' he kept saying.

Just to fill you in, comparatively few dogs will back sheep and those that do are highly-prized. A dog that is good in the paddock and also works well in the yards is known as a utility dog. They can command prices around $1000. We weren't about to sell the old chap, but it did turn out that there was to be an inaugural yard-dog event at the local show. Of course, Roy had to be entered.

'It's just a bit of fun,' we kept hearing. 'We won't get anywhere.'

But we did notice that the old dog was secretly being plied with duck eggs and milk, and more than once we heard the boss murmuring to him, 'Now you won't let me down, will you old man?' The boss believed the duck eggs would help his concentration and stamina.

So last Saturday, earlier than was good for us, we set off for the show. Roy's black coat was gleaming with all those duck eggs, but his tan eyebrows were drawn together slightly in puzzlement at all the fuss.

The showgrounds were still quiet when we arrived. The judging of cakes, flowers, showgirls and cattle had started and of course the horse events were in full swing. Around the yard-dog arena, a knot of dedicated dog people had gathered. A maze of yards had been set up, with a truck and a menacing-looking race leading to it.

The first competitors got under way—lean, professional-looking dogs, dispatching their sheep slickly into the truck. Then came the young dogs who found the whole occasion a bit of a romp. They raced and yapped and scattered sheep all over the ground, while their owners whistled and shouted and grew red in the face. The rules forbid swearing, otherwise I reckon we would have heard a bit of paddock language.

Roy, oblivious to the pressure on him, lay at the end of a piece of chain in the shade of the ute. The public address system in the distance was droning on, calling viewers for the showgirls, and announcing the winners of the classes of polished hacks. In the tin shed that served as the show pavilion there was excitement because the cornflour sponge had been won by a man. And my chocolate slice had scored. But there was no time for such frippery.

'Dog number 15,' said the man with the loud hailer in the dog ring—and the stomach butterflies surged and my palms sweated.

Roy and the boss strode into the ring. The boss looked a bit tense, but Roy was just looking around for some sheep to work. With the familiar command 'Go back', Roy leapt into action, brought the sheep into the yard and whizzed them down the race. The old boy even managed a few of his wheezy barks, and the spectators could see he was missing a few teeth.

The judges scribbled on bits of paper and the boss, sensing that things were going well, hissed between his teeth for Roy to 'Get up' on their backs. That would be the clincher—and after all, it was the whole reason we had brought the senile old fool.

But Roy wouldn't have a bar of it. He smiled up at the boss and wagged his tail to show he understood, then turned his back and went on with forcing the sheep up the race the way he had done it all his life. Nevertheless, although it was a good, clean display, we felt let down. We even felt a bit cheated that his new-found talent had been such a fleeting thing.

The judges sitting beneath their umbrellas on the back of a ute in the ring finished adding up the numbers. Up they went on the board.

'Crikey! The old fool has got into the finals!' we all shrieked.

And when the finals were over, Roy ended up in fourth place. It was all a bit of a thrill and old Roy danced around the boss as he was patted and fussed over like he never had been before. His tan eyebrows were still drawn together in puzzlement though. He thought he was only doing his job. Anyway, that night the old celebrity rode home in the front of the ute—something that had never happened before.

Now the boss says he'll try competing again, and he's excited about Roy and Rhubarb's pups which are due in a fortnight because he says, with such a champ for a father, they should be little beauties.

In the district even now there is talk of more yard-dog trials and who will take the laurels. The school is going to put on trials as part of its annual fundraiser and twenty blokes have got their names down. This is the new sport all right . . . and I suppose it's as good a way as any to distract us from the miserable spring rains and the fact that the crops are withering.

But all I'm worried about is whether I can keep up the supply of duck eggs.

FOLLOWING INSTINCTS

Roy Hentschke, Blyth

In the 1930s, a drover was given ten pounds to train a border collie pup for sheep work.

An uncle of mine rescued her from the drover who was beating her for disobedience. He swapped her with an uncontrollable no-hoper.

The bitch was called Minty. She was one of the best all-round sheepdogs I can remember.

When six years old, her former owner recognised her at the saleyards. My uncle immediately offered her back, but the former owner realised that if she had not been rescued from the drover, she may well have been dead. Instead, he said he would like a pup from her next litter.

When the litter of five pups arrived, Minty showed signs of sickness. When they were four weeks old, she carried them in her mouth, one by one, to a rabbit warren about 300 metres away.

My uncle returned them all to the kennel. He fed them and bedded them down.

The following day, the performance was repeated. Minty died not long after completing the task. This remarkable dog, knowing that death was imminent, had followed her instincts in making sure there was a source of food for her pups.

As a young farmer, I had one of her pups, Boxer, who became a good trial dog. I still have this blood line in my own dogs, fifty-two years later. They still have the 'eye' and ability that distinguished Minty.

GOODBYE LADY

Mrs John Schwarz, Taplan

His heart was heavy as he replaced the rifle behind the door. She had been a faithful companion for more than twelve years.

He had left it until almost dark, so that as the cold metal point touched her forehead, he wouldn't have to see those dark brown eyes of trust, imploring him for help.

It was during the last shearing, when she was on the back of the ute, heading out to bring in a new of mob of sheep, that a roll of barb wire, used for mending a fence the week before, had got entangled in the hair under her hind leg.

Part of the wire had cut into the bare patch of skin. The hair had to be cut, as well as the barb, to finally free Lady. The resulting wound never healed. Although she licked it daily to keep it clean, it always seemed to be weeping.

She seemed to lose the will to fight, and just lay waiting patiently, in a hole she had scratched for herself in the carport, beside the house. Barely eating, she would only lick at a dish of water. But she was alert to the end, always holding up her head, following keenly all the comings and goings of her friend, the boss.

He knew it was the kindest thing to do for her, but still he had put it off, hesitating to make the final break.

The boss wasn't the only one with a lump in his throat the next morning when he broke the news to the family. No longer would she be around when the ute was backed out of the shed. No longer would her warning bark be heard when a strange vehicle came up the track.

But later that day, Lady's freshly-weaned grandson rode in the ute on the boss's lap, to check the maiden ewes.

PART 8

A DOG'S BEST FRIEND

A DOG'S BEST FRIEND

Mike Hayes

Great store is always placed in the contribution working dogs make to the betterment of human existence. Although that's precisely what this book is about, it's time the tables were turned for a few pages. The human side of the partnership provides its own special characters, too.

Sheepdog trials are a sort of Cinderella sport in Australia. Their devotees are addicts of the first water, but the circle of followers is fairly small. Every Australian probably knows of their existence, but relatively few have experienced the genuine excitement of good competition. The trials' people themselves look wistfully to New Zealand where, they report mournfully, 'They have trials on prime time television.'

I became hooked on trials relatively recently when covering, for Countrywide, the big Bicentennial sheepdog competition held in conjunction with the Nationals at Hall, near Canberra, in 1988. It was there I first met George Westcott. The championship organiser spoke of George, a retired career public servant, with the awe other sports' fans reserve for a Don Bradman or Wally Lewis. The big difference is that George had never been a participant in his beloved sport—just an organiser—but arguably one of the most respected sports administrators in the land. The next time I met George was two years later at his outer Canberra home. He was mourning the loss of Polly, a seventeen-year-old retired sheepdog bitch he'd taken in twelve years earlier out of kindness rather than a desire to work with her.

'You know, when Polly died, my first thought was to go out immediately and get another dog. Then I realised I probably wouldn't be round for more than a couple of years,' George admitted.

So he reluctantly opted not to have another dog around the place. His bulky volumes of meticulously-kept records of the national sheepdog trials he stayed involved with for forty-five years have been turned over to the National Library.

'They keep trying to get me out of retirement to get involved in the Nationals again, but I'm not silly,' laughed George. He did all his work in an honorary capacity.

It struck me then that no coverage of Australian working dogs would be complete without a rather hefty reference to the sprightly bloke in his eighties who still seems to remember vividly every decent dog he's ever seen working and treasures the game's human characters like old wine.

'Funny thing . . . there never seems to have been any real rubbish in the trials game,' he muses. 'Oh, you'd occasionally see a bloke come in, shooting his mouth off and making himself unpopular—but give it a few years and he'd be gone. I don't know what it was. Perhaps it was the code of decency passed on by the old-timers, but those loud-mouthed fellers soon realised they weren't wanted.'

It was the day before Australia Day, 1990, and George confided quietly that he'd been officially notified he was going to be announced as an Order of Australia recipient. He'd already scored a Coronation Medal and the British Empire Medal for his public service.

'I don't know why they wanted to give me another gong,' he pretended to complain, clearly pleased at the latest honour and convinced that it really reflected the status of sheepdogs rather than bureaucrats. Dog trials are held all over Australia and, like all sports, produce arguments. There must be a thousand opinions on who really were the best dogs and probably just as many as to who contributed most to the sport.

I won't accept any arguments. George didn't invent sheepdog trials. They started in 1870 in Forbes, New South Wales, and were well-established in 1942 when George stuck his bib in and decided to organise a truly national competition. But no-one has worked so hard to promote the public awareness of that unique link between human and dog—so I'm nominating him as the 'Father' of the sport, and that's that.

George Westcott still chuckles about the first time he actually saw a sheepdog working. It was in 1920, in Kyabram, Victoria. George was only twelve at the time. His family had moved to the Goulburn Valley from Mirboo North, way down in damp Gippsland, after his dad, a small storekeeper, bought the local newsagency. Gippsland, especially around Mirboo North and at Boollara, where George went to school, wasn't sheep country.

'I don't think I'd even seen a sheep before we moved to Kyabram,' said George.

142

Their new house was slap-bang up against the wire fence around the Kyabram Showground. Such a prime location allowed young George to worm a hole in the fence and assure himself of lifetime free admission to the goings-on at the grounds. In 1920, at Kyabram's first agricultural show, George wriggled through his secret entrance and took in the sights. Suddenly an announcement crackled over the new loudspeaker system.

'I remember it saying that Mr Joseph Moses [father of future ABC chief Sir Charles Moses] of Tatura had agreed to give a demonstration of a working sheepdog,' George recalled. 'The people all formed a ring and old Mr Moses stood at the sidelines with a dog on a lead in one hand and a basket in the other. He put the basket down and, much to my surprise, took a beer tumbler out of his pocket and threw it into the middle of the ring. Then he opened the basket.'

Out stepped a rather confused rooster. If the rooster was perplexed at its situation, George was probably even more so. Even though he didn't know much about working dogs, he at least felt justified in expecting old Joe Moses to put his dog through its paces with sheep or cattle.

After letting the rooster get its bearings, Joe Moses gave his dog a pat and undid the clasp on its lead. Like the rest of the crowd, young George Westcott watched spellbound as the dog silently stalked the rooster, who was still trying to decide whether the wall of people encircling him might have some sort of exit through which he could escape.

'That dog worked the rooster round and round the ring,' said George. 'Round and round the beer glass. He didn't let up until that rooster finally stuck his head into the glass. That was it. The whole point of the demonstration was for that dog to get that rooster into the glass.'

It turned out that the trick was quite a common one among old-time dog handlers and it certainly whetted George's appetite to see and learn more about working dogs and subsequently, competitions.

Times change and, although he grew to appreciate the skills involved in his new-found interest, George's life was overtaken by the development of his own career. He joined the Public Service by winning a job at the Kyabram Post Office. In 1926,

Mr G Westcott, wet-behind-the-ears public servant, was shunted off to Canberra with another fledgling shiny-arse named Dick Casey [later Lord Casey, Governor General of Australia] and a truckload of official files to deliver them to the newly constructed government offices in West Block, not far from the spanking new Parliament House. Today, West Block still stands at the bureaucratic heart of the parliamentary triangle. However, when the two callow youths arrived with their precious cargo, they found, contrary to what they'd been assured by the staff of Prime Minister Stanley Melbourne Bruce, that it hadn't even been finished.

'The walls and roof were up but there wasn't a complete floor in the place—and the truck driver wanted the boxes carrying the files back so he could return to Melbourne for another load.'

A bureaucratic panic ensued and carpenters from building sites all over the national capital were press-ganged into service to install the floors quick smart.

'As the boards went down, we emptied more boxes of files,' recalls George.

The job was eventually completed and the truck driver left. But young George Westcott stayed in Canberra with those files—the first Commonwealth public servant to be transferred to the national capital.

Now none of that had anything to do with the working dogs, but it did put George in the right location for his later, self-appointed task of giving sheepdog trials a truly national home of their own. George went on over the subsequent decades to become one of the nation's most senior government administrators, spending his whole career in the Prime Minister's Department.

But diversions like careers are only the concern of mere humans. The fire rekindles in George Westcott's belly and his eyes get that far-away look not when he's reminiscing about government machinations but when he talks about dogs, handlers and competitors. It's interesting to note that George himself was never a handler with dogs and never competed—although he can deliver a curt 'Git behind' with all the authority of the best of them.

144

'I never actually had a go myself—but I could organise. That's how I got involved,' he maintained.

It was 1942, slap-bang in the middle of World War Two and the Treasurer of Legacy in Canberra, Eric Keage, asked George to come up with an idea for a fund raising function—and whatever he decided, could he also please organise it? George's mind drifted back to Joe Moses and the chook. He decided to try a working dog display and competition.

'A lot of people around Canberra had heard about working dogs, but I didn't think many of them had seen them,' he said.

The most desirable venue was Manuka Oval, and George fronted the guardians of its hallowed turf full of confidence in their generosity.

'They were horrified,' George recalls. 'Sheep? Someone was actually suggesting that sheep, with those sharp little hoofs, be allowed to trample all over their lovely turf cricket pitch?'

George's great scheme appeared doomed from the start. What was a born organiser—an expert administrator—expected to do in a situation like that? He did the only thing he could under the circumstances. He lied. What was all the worry about sheep on the turf wicket? Why, he knew from first-hand experience that the Sydney Cricket ground Trust actually owned a mob of sheep. And he'd often seen them grazing contentedly on *that* Hallowed Turf.

George maintains that it really wasn't all that much of a lie—just a little white one. But what did it matter? It worked. The first Canberra Sheep Dog Championships were held the following year at Manuka Oval, and continued there for many years.

'That first one was a pretty rough old sheepdog trial,' recalls George, somewhat ruefully. 'I knew a few people round here, and some over round Yass and Goulburn, who worked dogs and they said they'd be happy to take part. We even scraped together $150 in prize money, which was pretty good for the time. We named it the Canberra Championships, but that really didn't mean a thing. However, it did the trick.'

The 'trick' resulted in a cheque for $400 being handed over to Legacy—again quite a princely sum in 1942. Its success led to a decision to make the championships an annual event.

As anyone who's been involved in dog trials—or any other sport for that matter—will know, nothing ever runs perfectly. That first Canberra trial also heralded the local birth of that well-known bedfellow of dog competition—controversy. A major row broke out.

Tom South of Goulburn, New South Wales, working with Drummer, was the last competitor on the day and actually notched up a winning score. Straight away Major Doug McMaster, whose dog Dusty Bob had been leading until then, lodged a protest. According to the Major, Tom South had been using a stick over 18 inches long to direct Drummer. Out came the measuring tape. Tom's stick proved to be an illegal 22 inches long. Protest upheld.

'It didn't take long for word to get around, either,' remembers George. 'The next trials saw the old measuring tape being called for all over the place. But eventually, it died down.'

The 18 inch (or 45 cm) rule is one of the little regulations in a dog trial that can bring the unwary undone. George says the rule doesn't really cause many problems. 'Everyone knows about it. It's the responsibility of the handler and that seems to be about it.'

The rules for a dog trial are universal. There are two major categories of event in a trial—the Maiden and the Open—although in recent years the National has included a class for Improvers. The Maiden is restricted to dogs who've never won a trial. The Open, as the name says, is open to all comers, including dogs qualified for the Maiden. Improvers are midway between those categories, having won a Maiden but not an Open. Generally, Opens and Maidens are judged on the basis of two performances by each handler-dog team in the arena, although many championships, for various reasons, have been decided on a single run.

The villains of any dog trial are the sheep. Each competitor works a fresh mob of three sheep. According to the handlers, the success of a competitor can depend entirely on the mob. The term 'bastard of a mob' refers to sheep who just won't cooperate. The opposite term 'bloody beautiful mob' is rarely heard.

Each trial has a time limit of fifteen minutes. In that time the handler has to guide the dog, either by voice, whistle or

146

hand signals, through a series of tasks based upon standard paddock work. The dog's first job is to bring the mob back to the handler, who stands in an imaginary semicircle, from which he's not allowed to move during the first task, on pain of instant disqualification.

The handler and the dog wait ready, with the dog behind the human. At the peal of the starting bell, the dog is sent to the other end of the field where the sheep have been released. Ideally it should be a wide, pear-shaped cast, with the dog stopping at just the right spot without spooking the mob. A good dog will hold the sheep until they settle down, confident that they aren't going to get their throats ripped out. If the sheep look like breaking away from the dog, he has to be positioned to stop them. If they look like going the other way, the trick is to pull the dog up short to block them. It's essential that the dog reacts to the handler's commands instantly—a second or two either way could cruel the whole move.

In this early phase, the dog has to bring the sheep in a straight line back to the handler and hold them in the imaginary circle behind him. Only when that's done can the handler move from his ring. He then moves to the next obstacle—the race—and positions himself again within a restricted area. Keeping the sheep on the correct side of a line of flags, the dog moves them to the race. If he's taken the initiative and jumped the gun— moving the sheep through the race before the boss gets there— well, too bad. He'll just have to repeat the manoeuvre once the handler's reached his possie.

After the race, a similar task has to be performed moving the sheep across a small bridge. Again the boss has to operate from within a ring. Finally, the sheep have to be penned. Not until they're all in can the handler close the gate behind them and await the judge's decision. In the middle of all of it, the team can be disqualified not only if the human side of the partnership leaves the ring, but if the dog ever crosses between either one, some or all of the sheep and the handler.

The handler and dog start each trial with a clear sheet of 100 points. As they progress around the course, points are deducted for errors and even something as nebulous as the 'quality of work'.

'You might get a handler who doesn't actually break the

rules, but gives the appearance that he's skating on thin ice, seeing just how far he can go. You can get points deducted for that,' advised George. 'Or if a judge thinks a handler's obviously lairising. I've had a beer with a judge after a trial and he'll say to me 'I know which dog I'd like to take home with me.' It sometimes turns out to be a dog that didn't get anywhere in the competition. He just wasn't being worked right. The worker lost all the points. One bloke who actually did well and got a lot of publicity, let it go to his head. He couldn't work out why he didn't do well. But you see, although he was getting his name in the paper and everything, whenever he competed, he tended to lairise, and the judges marked him down for that.'

In 1945, the title of the Canberra championships was changed and the first National Sheep Dog Trials Championships were run at Manuka. It followed a visit the previous year to the oval by the Duke and Duchess of Gloucester. The Duke, then Governor General, was so impressed by what he'd seen, he invited George back to Yarralumla for a viceregal chat. The Duke didn't muck about. He asked George how he could help in future trials. Never backward in coming forward, George suggested the GG donate a sash for his new brainchild—a national sheepdog trial to be held annually in the national capital. His simple fundraising exercise now had viceregal patronage or—considering His Royal Highness's position as brother to King George—real royal patronage.

That historic first National Championship was judged by Arthur Collins of 'Lucindale', South Australia, and won by Nayook Moss, owned by Dr RB Kelly and worked by Jack Donnelly of Bungendore, New South Wales. The sudden emergence of what many regarded as George Westcott's private circus put a few noses out of joint, especially in Victoria where the dog trials establishment considered *their* state was the true home of national competition.

'Some Victorians complained they were actually scrubbed by their organisation down there when they came up here, but eventually word got around and soon they were all taking part in the Canberra Nationals.'

George recalls the 1946-52 period as the era of the kelpies at the National. It was during this time that the dog considered

148

by many, including George Westcott, to be the finest ever to compete, starred in the competition. Johnny was a large black and tan kelpie, out of Warragul by Scarlet O'Hara. He was bred by CL Walker of Tenterfield, New South Wales, but owned and worked by Athol Butler of Moree, New South Wales. He competed in five national Open championships and won the lot. To George, Johnny's greatest moment occurred when he competed with a huge gash inside one of his back legs.

'Athol Butler turned up shaking his head and saying he didn't think Johnny would compete,' recalled George. 'He ripped his leg jumping over a fence. It needed five stitches. He'd been lying down ever since, obviously distressed and not even looking as though he could go out onto the course.

'Athol was a real gentleman—the sort of bloke you'd always be glad to invite into your home. He was really worried about Johnny. During the day, you'd miss him and go looking for him. You'd find him back with Johnny, feeding him raw egg and Johnny looking as though he wouldn't be able to stand, let alone compete.

'I told Athol, 'Look, I'll get a vet to give him a needle. If the vet says he shouldn't compete, then we'll pull him out of the trials.' The vet gave Johnny the needle and then stayed to make sure he was all right.'

That was in 1952, when Johnny took out the Open with his highest score—197 points.

'He was such a good competitor that he developed an avid following,' said George. 'They used to call a stop to the Easter tennis championships at the Manuka courts, just over the road from the Oval, so the players could come over and watch Johnny compete.

'In my honest opinion, I believe that great dog was at least five points per run superior to any sheepdog that I witnessed working in the National Championships during my forty-five years associated with the trials. No old-time trial worker has questioned my opinion.'

Since then, George has seen dogs compete well after such diverse handicaps as nursing injuries from a pre-trial brawl, or only a short time after retrieving flood-stranded mobs on their rain-drenched home properties. Trial dogs are, after all, mainly workaday dogs as well. But he still lists Johnny as the greatest.

149

'You only have to look at his record. Not only did he scoop the pool but he actually improved his score in the Open each year:

1946   90-90=180 pts
1947   94-88 =182 pts
1948   93-90 =183 pts
1951   97-95 =192 pts
1952   97-100=197 pts

Johnny died in 1959, aged 17.'

Year by year, the National became stronger in terms of truly Australia-wide competition. In 1947, for the first time, the South Australians JB Walsh and W Crozer took part, along with the Kiwis Harry Harris and PG McKenzie. Harris came back fifteen times and won the National in 1965 with Lucky.

Money in sport has always been a controversial issue, but people generally recognise now that, the pro-am argument aside, a certain amount of cash is always needed just to run things properly and provide some incentive for top competitors. In George's own words, the trial workers throughout Australia were 'dumbfounded' when, in 1950, he announced that the prize money for the next National would be $3500. That was at least three times that of any previous purse in the world. Today, the National offers prizes worth between $7000 and $12,000 and George believes it will soon be $25,000.

1951 was the Commonwealth Jubilee Year. As if to mark the occasion, for the first time, all states were represented in that year's National. One hundred and forty-three dogs competed and trophies were donated by the Duke of Gloucester, the Governor General Sir William McKell, the Commonwealth Government and the High Commissions of the UK, Canada, New Zealand, South Africa, India, Ceylon and Pakistan, the International Sheep Dog Society of England, Scotland and Wales, the All-Ireland Collie and Sheep Dog Society and many Australian businesses.

In 1952, George was elected an honorary Life Member of the National Sheep Dog Trials Association. That was also the year Archie Hudson of Cobar, New South Wales, broke the time record by completing the course with Panda in 6 minutes 48½ seconds—only to see it beaten a few trials later by Gerald Nightingale when he completed his round with Barney in 6 minutes 8 seconds.

1953, and the National Association ran its first-ever dog auction. Thirty-eight dogs changed hands for 760 guineas. They included the champion kelpie Silver, offered by Tony Mongan of Buffalo River South, Victoria. Silver was bought by a partnership of Parson and Martin for 190 guineas. That year Donald Smith of Surat, Queensland, won his first National Open with Kennie. That was also when George scored his first official honour—the Coronation Medal—in recognition of his service to the Government.

In 1954 the National Association tried to organise the first truly international competition in Australia by inviting the sheepdog trial associations in England, Scotland, Wales, Ireland and New Zealand to compete in a proposed championship during the 1956 Melbourne Olympic Games. It even offered to contribute towards the expense of bringing in dogs and handlers. However, quarantine regulations torpedoed the scheme.

That year's National started dramatically when, at 6 am on opening day, George received a phone call to say the judge, James Moore of West Wyalong, New South Wales, had been found dead in his bed at the Kingston Hotel in Canberra. Panic ensued. An unsuspecting Don Ross, from Korrumburra in Victoria, was quietly strolling through the front gate at Manuka Oval, looking forward to being a spectator at his first National, when the legions of Westacott pounced. Don found himself elevated to the position of Official Judge. He officiated in declaring Alan Miller of Woodend, Victoria, the winner of the Open with his border collie Kyneton Afton (who also won in 1955).

The issue of whether good working dogs and trials dogs are bred, trained or the result of some miracle of nature will always be contentious talking points among Those In The Know (and Those Who Reckon They're In The Know). Many dog breeders will swear blind they've wasted a lifetime trying to extract talented progeny from champion dogs without success. However, Miller's association with the Nationals seems to indicate that there's definitely something in the breeding.

151

His wins in 1954 and 1955 obviously increased interest in the 1955 dog auction, when seventeen dogs sold for 810 guineas. The top price was 215 guineas, paid by Mrs Jean Beatson of Yea, Victoria, for the great border collie bitch Gowrie Sheila and six pups sired by Macroy (Imp.) on behalf of Chris Howe of Mooroopna, Victoria. Gowrie Sheila was the mother of two future National double-winners, Herdsmen's Wee Dell and Miller's Kyneton Afton. Miller and Kyneton Afton made their mark on the 1956 National. Miller (who George has nearly convinced himself was the best handler he'd ever seen) took out his third National with Luck, at the same time gaining second place with Jill. Both dogs and the third place-getter had been sired by Kyneton Afton.

That Olympic year saw the launch of the largest sheepdog competition circuit in Australia. George and Joe Byrne of Bourke, New South Wales, put together a series of trials which started in Canberra and took in Wellington, Nyngan, Cobar and Bourke.

The 1957 National was notable because it was the only occasion a husband and wife team did the judging. Archie Hudson of Cobar did the honours in the Open while his wife Maisie officiated during the Maiden. Maisie went on to judge the 1960 Open. 1957 was also the year Herdsmen's Wee Dell won her first National Open for Bill Marshall of Tatura, Victoria. The Maiden went to Tom Wilmot of Alexandria, Victoria, with Black, bred by the President of the National Association, Fred Southwell.

The 1957 auction saw twenty-two dogs sold for £833. Trevor Mooring of Bourke paid a then-record price of 300 guineas for Cheviot Speed. Acting on behalf of W Van Dyl of Cape Province, South Africa, George Westcott purchased two kelpie pups from Chris Howe of Mooroopna. They were believed to be the first Australian kelpies to be sent to South Africa.

Major sponsorship emerged for the National for the first time in 1958. The Vacuum Oil Company agreed to sponsor the Association. It was a relationship that lasted fifteen years and helped make the organisation perhaps the most respected and largest sheepdog body in the world. The level of international respect continued to grow. In 1961 George drew up the constitution, rules and course layout for a South African clone

152

of the National Association and arranged the trophies and a judge for its first championships.

In 1964 George won his next gong—the BEM for his public service.

In 1966 the second contender for George's accolade as the Best Worker (handler) in Australia entered the competition. He was Geoff Jolly of Derrinallume, Victoria. Geoff became the first trials handler to win both the Open and Maiden in the same year. Moroko Spark, with 91–80 points won the Open and Moroko Lil (92), the Maiden. Geoff went on to win a record of six National Opens.

'I found Jolly always fascinating to watch,' recalled George. 'Once a trial started, he'd wander off on his own and watch the other competitors working. You'd automatically think he was checking out the competition, but that wasn't the case. Actually, he'd be appraising the sheep. After a while he'd come back and say, "Ohhh, they're a terrible lot of sheep . . . but I've got just the dog to handle them.'

'He'd judge the sheep and then select the dog he'd use to beat them. And he'd usually be right. Jolly usually had eight or twelve dogs with him whenever he went to compete.'

Over the years, George has always admitted it's been a toss-up between Geoff and his old mate Alan Miller as to who was top of the heap. He generally returns to Miller as the out-and-out master. 'There's no doubt that Miller taught Jolly and that's what gives him the edge.'

Despite Geoff's unique talent of fitting the dog to the sheep, Miller had the singular ability to rectify his mistakes.

'He could make an error on the arena and correct it to his advantage, therefore only losing the minimum number of points. If you chipped him about it, he'd make you think he'd done the whole thing—including the mistake—deliberately.

'Miller used to say some terrible things to Geoff. Jolly was a fiery sort of bloke away from trials, but he'd quieten right down when he came to Canberra for the National. He never went off when Miller had a go at him. He always respected him. Often when the trials were on, Geoff would ask out of the blue if he could come around for a yarn. "I just want to get away from that Alan Miller," he'd say jokingly.

'Jolly died not long back, but Miller's still living in a nursing home. I keep in touch with him and see him now and then. The poor old bloke can't get around much and his sight's fading, but you should see his eyes light up when we start talking about dogs and trials.'

In 1967 the government accepted George's suggestion that Australian sheepdogs should be a feature of Expo 67 in Montreal. Alan Miller and his two collies Rifton Cobber and Herdsman Jewell were the selected ambassadors. According to George, Miller became the first sportsman to be televised throughout the world via satellite when he gave his exhibition on Australia Day.

1970 marked the centenary of sheepdog trials in Australia. Just for the record, that first trial was won by a black and tan kelpie bitch called King's Kelpie. She was by Caesar out of Gleeson's Kelpie. Her pups were called Kelpie's pups and before long, the name was shortened simply to Kelpies and applied to all of that fine breed. The original kelpies, of course, were Celtic water sprites.

In 1970, the Queen and Prince Phillip presented the trophies at the National. The National Open champions were Bob Ross of Korrumburra, Victoria, with Yulong Russ and the special Centenary Open was won by Gordon Young of Dulacca, Queensland, with Minto Gael.

In 1975, Her Majesty gave permission for a perpetual trophy in her name. The royal connection with the trials continued in 1977, when approval was given for the presentation of a Special Silver Jubilee Trophy, won by John Elliott of Gundagai, New South Wales.

By 1982, prize money had increased at the Nationals to $12,000—a far cry from the original $150 offered back in 1942 at Manuka Oval. The lucky Open winner was Ross Dodge of Waaring, Victoria, with Whalma Sam.

In 1984, the largest sheepdog trial ever run drew fifty-six competitors from all states, with 221 dogs (including thirty-four all the way from Western Australia) making up 766 entries overall. Clarrie Camin of Sale, Victoria, won the Open with Rosemount Louise.

In 1986 George pulled the pin. Because of ill-health, he announced his retirement as founder, Life Member, and forty-five years as National Association honorary secretary. Apart from

having enjoyed sharing the skill and comradeship of th
hundreds of dogs and workers he'd seen in that time, Georg
talks with quiet pride of his own efforts, not on the arena,
but behind the scenes. From that original £150 scraped together
forty-eight years earlier for his inaugural 'Rough old trial', he
feels he achieved his goal of ensuring the National always ran
in a businesslike way and points with satisfaction to the
$47,000 the Association's managed to invest to ensure its
economic future.

'I always made sure I kept our sponsors informed about what
was going on. I didn't just write to them once a year asking
for donations. I'd write regularly, giving them all the latest
news. That way they knew they were part of the Nationals
and wanted to stay involved. A lot of the heads of some of
Australia's biggest companies have admitted to me that they
used to say, 'God! Not another letter from old George Westcott.'
But they continued to support us and a lot of them talked
proudly about their association with sheepdog trials in their
own write-ups.'

George Westcott admits he's in the late twilight of his years and talks
openly about wanting to die in Canberra, the city he loves. The last
time I left him, he agreed to send me his records of the various Nationals
winners.

'I've got them all typed up somewhere,' he grumbled, 'but I can't quite
put my hands on it.

'I knocked it together years ago when ads started appearing in the
paper offering pups for sale. They'd always include something like:
'Winner of the National Open in 1958'. I knew darn well who'd won
that year, and whatever dog they were trying to advertise—well, I'd
never heard of it in my life.

'So I drew up the full list. I've had scores of requests for it all the
time. I reckon it settles a few arguments.'

He talked again of Polly, the ancient sheepdog who'd died only
a couple of weeks earlier. 'You know, when we moved back here
from the coast, she wandered out onto the road and I just said: 'Go
back' and she came in. She only ever needed to be told once. She
hadn't worked for ages but she could still tell, after all these years,
when you meant what you said.'

...George feels he hasn't the time to take on another

...ckety old campaigner retired from the arena or the

...ey'd have so much in common and all dogs deserve

...ke George. A bloke like him's very important in our world

...unlike those of us who virtually have to rely on our dogs,

...has dedicated his life to them—and their human hangers-

...imply out of love.

...ere's his list.

NATIONAL SHEEP DOG TRIALS ASSOCIATION CANBERRA

Author's note: I've taken these records directly from George's typed notes. There are some omissions in relation to full details, especially during the 1970s, but the basic results are still there. Sadly, there's a huge hole where the National results for the mid to late eighties should be. It's probably a result of George's heavy almost lone work as honorary secretary for so long. When he retired and moved for a short time to the south coast of New South Wales from Canberra (he soon returned), some of his meticulously kept files were apparently lost. Despite searches by the current honorary secretary, Margaret Hunter, those missing files are still just that. Maybe they'll turn up again one day. In the meantime, my apologies to those worthy dogs and workers (handlers) who won during those years.

In reworking the records, I've just given the first three place-getters in each event, purely because of space restrictions. However, I think the information here is enough to let us all know who the top dogs and workers (handlers) have been in the Nationals and enables us to plot the fortunes of top players like Geoff Jolly, whose record in the mid-seventies is nothing short of amazing—with his 'protégé' Ross Dodge not far behind him. According to George, the Moroko line of dogs who feature so prominently in this record—especially with Jolly—were considered the top breed in Victoria. If there are slight hiccups in the spelling of some dogs' names, it's because that's how they appeared in the records. If anyone's miffed by the odd wrong letter here and there, I apologise. On the other hand, it does nothing to diminish the records set by those great canine competitors, so you shouldn't get too upset. Spelling and names are really the boring concern of humans, after all.

157

1943

Open   Judge: J Donnelly (all events, both years)

1st	D McMaster	Dusty Bob	182 pts (on protest)
2nd	T South	Drummer	184 pts
3rd	T South	Jed	169 pts

Maiden

1st	T South	Beat	159 pts
2nd	D Tully	Flo	146 pts
3rd	H Lawton	Blue Boy	126 pts

1944

Open

1st	T South	Jed	173 pts
2nd	D McMaster	Dusty Bob	163 pts
3rd	A Bolton	Maisie	160 pts

Maiden

1st	T South	Mack	180 pts
2nd	J Morrison	Tralee Rose	156 pts
3rd	T South	Jeff	139 pts

1945

Open   Judge: A Collins

1st	R B Kelly	Moss	88-90=178 pts
2nd	I Price	Irvale Don	88-89=177 pts
3rd	J Morrison	Tralee Rose	83-89=172 pts

1946

Maiden   Judge: R C Noakes

1st	D Tully	Flo	81-61=142 pts
2nd	T South	Kemp	73-65=138 pts
3rd	J Moore	Jeanne	70-58=128 pts

Open   Judge: M A McLeod

1st	A Butler	Johnny	90-90=180 pts
Eq. 2nd	T South	Jeff	95-77=172 pts
	R B Kelly &		
	D Russell	Herdsman Fleet	90-82=172 pts

1947

Open   Judge: R C Noakes

1st	A Butler	Johnny	94-88=182 pts
2nd	J B Walsh	The Major	89-90=179 pts
3rd	T South	Beadavale	90-78=168 pts

1948

Open Judge: A D Anson
1st	A Butler	Johnny	93-90=183 pts
2nd	H H Harris	Border Fay	87-89=176 pts
3rd	A E Meacham	Kyneton Glennie	79-73=152 pts

1950

Open Judge: R C Noakes
1st	C W Butt	Curly	87-86=173 pts
2nd	G Stanyer	Blue Bonnett	89-74=163 pts
3rd	A E Meacham	Wyalong Torley	89-68=157

1951

Open Judge: J Batson
1st	A Butler	Johnny	97-95=192 pts
2nd	C W S McDonald	Ellardslea Judy	93-90=183 pts
3rd	A Meacham	Kyneton Lyn	92-90=182 pts

1952

Open Judge: R C Noakes
1st	A Butler	Johnny	97-100=197 pts
2nd	H H Harris	General Haigh	95-98=193 pts
3rd	L M Nugent	Kurrari Bonny	98-93=191 pts

Maiden
1st	D D Smith	Garry	90-83=174 pts
2nd	H Lawton	Red Boy	94-79=173 pts
3rd	A Hudson	Panda	87-84=171 pts

1953

Open Judge: C W S McDonald
1st	D D Smith	Kenny	93-95=188 pts
Eq 2nd	S McMaster	Mist	93-94=187 pts
	J Casey	Mick	94-93=187 pts

Maiden
1st	R Beatson	Firrhill Bracken	82-74=156 pts
2nd	D C Laird	Glencoe Betty	83-65=148 pts
3rd	A E Hudson	Julie	81-64=145 pts

1954

Open Judge: D Ross
1st	A Miller	Kyneton Afton	93-95=188 pts
2nd	S McMaster	Ned	94-93=187 pts
3rd	L M Nugent	Wanga Russ	91-93=184 pts

Maiden Judge: J Morrison
1st	R H Cox	Clytie's Sugar	90-85=175 pts
2nd	B O'Kane	Annandale Lance	94-73=167 pts
3rd	E Toomey	Rover	90-69=159 pts

1955

Open　Judge: F Pratley
1st	A Miller	Kyneton Afton	95-97=192 pts
2nd	H Harris	Bill	94-97=191 pts
3rd	L M Nugent	Wanga Russ	95-92=187 pts

Maiden　Judge: T Wright
1st	Mrs R Beatson	Firrhill Bob	82 pts Won on run off.
2nd	C McKenzie	Marilla Fairy	82 pts
3rd	Mrs R Beatson	Firrhill Soda	79 pts

1956

Open　Judge: D Ross
1st	A Miller	Luck	87-93=180 pts
2nd	A Miller	Jill	89-89=178 pts
3rd	R Bogie	Miller's Bob	86-85=171 pts

Maiden　Judge: F Widdicombe
1st	F J McIntosh	Lock Moy Lachlan	92 pts
2nd	F J Shannon	Clown	91 pts
3rd	A C Hearn	Herdsman Speedy Bill	87 pts

1957

Open　Judge: A E Hudson
1st	W R Marshall	Herdsmen's Wee Dell	98-98=196 pts
2nd	R R Shepherd	Fortune's Lass	99-96=195 pts
3rd	R W Bogie	Miller's Bob	98-96=194 pts

Maiden　Judge: Mrs M Hudson
1st	Tom Wilmot	Black	93 pts Won on run off
2nd	A C Hearn	Herdsman Speedy Bill	93 pts
3rd	R R Sandford	Argyle Blaze	92 pts

1958

Open　Judge: D D Smith
1st	E L Morris	Herdsman Charlie	92-91=183 pts
2nd	H H Harris	Bill	91-91=182 pts
3rd	J W Grady	Karringal Don	91-84=175 pts

Maiden　Judge: F J McIntosh
1st	D D Smith	Kennie Junior	91 pts
2nd	A C Hearne	Flockman Junetta	86 pts
3rd	N Wettenhall	Inverbrackie Snip	84 pts

160

1959

Open   Judge: A Miller
1st		W R Marshall	Herdsmen's Wee Dell	91–93=184 pts
2nd		R W Bogie	Navarre Flash	91–90=181 pts
3rd		T Wilmot	Smoke	90–89=179 pts

Maiden   Judge: C W Butt
1st		G Brennan	Bruce 11	95 pts
2nd		D Tully	Fleet	92 pts
3rd		A Miller	Gaffer	91 pts

1960

Open   Judge: Mrs M Hudson
1st		B O'Kane	Yarramine Whisky	91–87=178 pts
2nd		W R Marshall	Herdsmen's Wee Dell	94–80=174 pts
3rd		F J McIntosh	Bellevue Don	95–72=167 pts

Maiden   Judge: H Lawton
1st		R W Bogie	Austral Shep	87 pts
2nd		E Morris	Nayook Trix	85 pts
3rd		G Thornton	Kyneton Tramp	84 pts

1961

Open   Judge: C W Butt
1st		G Kenny	Kialla Panda	96–97=193 pts
2nd		B O'Kane	Yarramine Collingwood	93–90=183 pts
3rd		H H Harris	Chips	95–87=182 pts

Maiden   Judge: R W Bogie
1st		A Miller	Miller's Pete	96 pts
2nd		B O'Kane	Yarramine Collingwood	94 pts
3rd		W E Wickam	Paroo Von	91 pts

1962

Open   Judge: F J McIntosh
1st		C L Camin	Alroy Wearie Willie	87–76=163 pts
2nd		G L Jolly	Kurrari Buck	79–61=140 pts
3rd		C L Camin	Alroy Count Again	84–46=130 pts

Maiden   Judge: R R Shephard
1st		A Miller	Miller's Clyde	90 pts
2nd		E Middleton	Morrison's Gwen	89 pts
3rd		H C Vincent	Dan	86 pts

161

1963

Open Judge: W R Marshall

1st	E L Morris	Koonda Jean	95-95=190 pts
2nd	R W Bogie	Alroy Rusty	92-95=187 pts
3rd	H H Harris	Lucky	92-94=186 pts

Maiden Judge: H Lawton

1st	R Sandford	Eulo Boxer	75 pts
2nd	E L Morris	Nayook Buster	71 pts
Eq 3rd	A E Gray	Herdsman's Donnie	70 pts
	A Miller	Ken	70 pts

1964

Open Judge: D Smith

1st	W R Marshall	Wooroona Bill	93-93=186 pts
2nd	J Harriott	Jet	93-92=185 pts
3rd	H Gibson	Vervale Mitzi	92-91=183 pts

Maiden Judge: J Morrison

1st	L Armstrong	Prince	97 pts
2nd	E L Morris	Nayook Buster	96 pts
Eq 3rd	R R Sandford	Argyle Paddy	95 pts
	E Sage	Sage's Pipsy	95 pts

1965

Open Judge: H Gibson

1st	H H Harris	Lucky	95-95=190 pts
2nd	W R Marshall	Minto Susie 2nd	91-87=178 pts
3rd	E L Morris	Koonda Jean	91-86=177 pts

Maiden Judge: H C Vincent

1st	G L Jolly	Strathearn Connie	96 pts
Eq 2nd	E Middleton	Penmore Penny	95 pts
	C Camin	Rocky Roy	95 pts

1966

Open Judge: A Miller

1st	G J Jolly	Moroko Spark	91-89=189 pts
2nd	E Middleton	Penmore Penny	90-83=173 pts
3rd	H Gibson	Vervale Mitzi	89-83=172 pts

Maiden Judge: B O'Kane

1st	G L Jolly	Moroko Lil	92 pts on run off
2nd	R R Sandford	Argyle Gyp	92 pts
Eq 3rd	H Gibson	Rosemont Sky	90 pts
	W Ryan	Collydale Tim	90 pts

1967

Open Judge: E L Morris

1st	W R Marshall	Herdsman's Gem	92–86=178 pts
2nd	J B Walsh	Verjimar Battle	92–82=174 pts
3rd	C Camin	Camin's Cactus	92–79=171 pts

Maiden Judge: J Nancarrow

1st	G L Jolly	Herdsman's Maggie	94 pts
Eq 2nd	G L Jolly	Moroko Heather	93 pts
	R R Sandford	Argyle Gyp	93 pts

1968

Open Judge: D Ross

1st	E Sage	Herdsman's Kenny	92–90=182 pts
2nd	R Sandford	Killoran Tally Hi	90–86=176 pts
3rd	W R Marshall	Mackie	92–81=173 pts

Maiden Judge: D Ross

1st	G L Jolly	Moroko Tess	82–86=168 pts
2nd	C Exton	Linton Pete	83–83=166 pts
3rd	H Lawton	Meg	85–78=163 pts

1969

Open Judge: O F Fish

1st	G L Jolly	Camin's Cactus	92–88=180 pts
2nd	B Quarrell	Quarrell's Jill	90–79=169 pts
3rd	R Ross	Yulong Russ	92–75=167 pts

Maiden Judge: G Young

1st	G L Jolly	Scout	157 pts

1970

Open

1st	R Ross	Yulong Russ

Centenary Open

1st	G Young	Minto Gal

Maiden

1st	Mrs P Atkins	Borcol Mirk's Girl	189 pts

Centenary Maiden

1st	Mrs P Atkins	Borcol Mirk's Girl	96 pts

163

1971

Open
1st   G L Jolly   Austral Blaze   187 pts

Maiden
1st   G L Jolly   Gidgee   180 pts

1972

Open
1st   B O'Kane   Moorland Lou   180 pts

Maiden
1st   G L Jolly   Camin's Juan   168 pts

1973

Open
1st   L Armstrong   Alphadale Scottie   184 pts

Improvers
1st   G L Jolly   Wyoming Kathy   92 pts

Maiden
1st   E Sage   Sage's Tiny   173 pts

1974

Open
1st   R Dodge   Rocky   189 pts

Improvers
1st   J Griffith   Kurrajong Bounce   92 pts

Maiden
1st   K Daltry   Yarramine Chips   181 pts

1975

FIRST AUSTRALIAN SEAT OF GOVERNMENT CHAMPIONSHIPS

Open   Judge: G L Jolly
1st   J Nevett   Astronaut Glen   91 pts
2nd   D Smith   Herdsman
                                        Wee Gem   89 pts
Eq 3rd   A N Scott   Paroo Rad   88 pts
                    L Walsh   Torana Fly 2nd   88 pts

Improvers   Judge: G L Jolly
1st   L Walsh   Torana Fly 2nd   88 pts
2nd   B Rayner   Dodge's Speed   86 pts
Eq 3rd   M Forrest   Narioka Jill   83 pts
                    J Hiscock   Millar's Mighty   83 pts

164

1st	G L Jolly	Moorlands Cap	95 pts
Eq 2nd	J Hiscock	Moorlands Don	93 pts
	J Varena	Eastgrove Gundy	93 pts

1976

NATIONAL CHAMPIONSHIPS

Open   Judge: A J Bromhan

1st	G L Jolly	Moorlands Gem	95-95=189 pts
2nd	G L Jolly	Moroko Twig	89-88=177 pts
3rd	A N Scott	Paroo Rad	90-83=173 pts

Improvers   Judge: A J Bromhan

1st	G L Jolly	Moroko Twig	89-76=165 pts
2nd	G L Jolly	Moroko Fox	86-76=162 pts
3rd	G L Jolly	Moorlands Gem	97-disqualified =97 pts

Maiden   Judge: J Griffiths

1st	G L Jolly	Miller's Freckles	88-69=157 pts
2nd	G L Jolly	Moroko Shack	79-66=145 pts
3rd	D M Rattray	Lyster Lass	73-48=121 pts

AUSTRALIAN SEAT OF GOVERNMENT CHAMPIONSHIPS

Open   Judge: A J Bromham

1st	G Jolly	Moorlands Gem	95 pts
Eq 2nd	A N Scott	Paroo Rad	90 pts
	R Dodge	Moroko Spring	90 pts

Improvers   Judge: A J Bromham

1st	G L Jolly	Moorlands Gem	95 pts
2nd	G L Jolly	Moroko Twig	89 pts
3rd	G L Jolly	Moroko Fox	86 pts

Maiden   Judge: J Griffith

1st	G L Jolly	Miller's Freckles	88 pts
2nd	G L Jolly	Moroko Shack	79 pts
3rd	G L Jolly	Moroko Springtime	72 pts

1977

NATIONAL CHAMPIONSHIPS

Open   Judge: D Smith

1st	L Armstrong	Alphadale Kim	183 pts
2nd	B Doyle	Kynoona Spark	178 pts
3rd	W Gow	Gowanbrae Jane	175 pts

165

Improvers   Judge: D Smith
1st	L Armstrong	Alphadale Kim	172 pts
2nd	R Dodge	Dodge's Kite	165 pts
3rd	J Harrington	Stevo' Star	156 pts

Maiden   Judge: R Dodge
1st	L Armstrong	Alphadale Tex	167 pts
2nd	B Doyle	Kynoona Sally	161 pts
3rd	A J Bromham	Grenville Jean	155 pts

AUSTRALIAN SEAT OF GOVERNMENT CHAMPIONSHIPS

Open
1st	R Dodge	Dodge's Kite	94 pts
2nd	M Saward	Stockman's Penny	92 pts
3rd	B Doyle	Kynoona Spark	91 pts

Improvers
1st	R Dodge	Dodge's Kite	94 pts
2nd	L Armstrong	Alphadale Kim	89 pts
3rd	W Carr	Rocky Barr Ripper	87 pts

Maiden
1st	B Doyle	Kynoona Sally	84 pts
2nd	A J Bromham	Grenville Jean	82 pts
3rd	R Hutchins	Moroko Dell	78 pts

Champion of Champion's Trophy: M Saward with Stockman's Penny, 92 pts

QUEEN'S SILVER JUBILEE SPECIAL NATIONAL OPEN

Judge: A J Bromham
1st	J Elliott	Olive Farm Banjo	173 pts
2nd	B Doyle	Kynoona Spark	170 pts
3rd	R Dodge	Dodge's Paddington	168 pts

1978

NATIONAL CHAMPIONSHIPS

Open   Judge: H Ashcroft
1st	G L Jolly	Moorland Blaze	189 pts
2nd	B Doyle	Kynoona Matt	179 pts
3rd	D Rattray	Lyster Lass	176 pts

Improvers
1st	G L Jolly	Moorland Blaze	177 pts
2nd	W Carr	Wamstead Scamp	161 pts
3rd	B O'Kane	Bashford's Toss	146 pts

166

Maiden   Judge: L Noble

1st	R Dodge	Moroko Arch	155 pts
2nd	R Dodge	Dutson Mandy	149 pts
3rd	G L Jolly	Twilight	140 pts

AUSTRALIAN SEAT OF GOVERNMENT CHAMPIONSHIPS

Open

1st	G L Jolly	Moorland Blaze	96 pts
Eq 2nd	B O'Kane	Bashford's Toss	91 pts
	D Rattray	Lyster Lass	91 pts

Improvers

1st	G L Jolly	Moorland Blaze	96 pts
2nd	B O'Kane	Bashford's Toss	91 pts
3rd	W Carr	Wamstead Scamp	86 pts

Maiden

1st	R Dodge	Dutson Mandy	89 pts
2nd	G L Jolly	Twilight	88 pts
Eq 3rd	D Smith	Barrackdale Pal	87 pts
	R Dodge	Moroko Arch	87 pts

Champion of Champions Trophy: C Exton with Linton Pete, 66 pts.

1979

NATIONAL CHAMPIONSHIPS

Open   Judge: J Griffith

1st	J Elliott	Olive Park Banjo	144 pts
2nd	A N Scott	Paroo Rad	143 pts
3rd	B O'Kane	Bashford's Toss	141 pts

Improvers

1st	B O'Kane	Bashford's Toss	132 pts
2nd	G L Jolly	Moorland Joe	119 pts
3rd	R Dodge	Moroko Arch	78 pts

Maiden   Judge: L Armstrong

1st	J Dodge	Dodge's Boxer	108 pts
2nd	R Dodge	Dodge's Paddington	101 pts
3rd	W Carr	Tip	80 pts

ARNOTTS SPILLER'S CHAMPIONSHIPS

Open

1st	G L Jolly	Moorland Blaze	88 pts
2nd	A N Scott	Paroo Rad	85 pts
3rd	B O'Kane	Camin's Anyhow	84 pts

167

Improvers

1st	R Dodge	Moroko Arch	78 pts
2nd	G L Jolly	Moorland Joe	76 pts
3rd	A N Dwyer	Lyster Glenelg	72 pts

Maiden

1st	J Dodge	Dodge's Boxer	83 pts
2nd	W Carr	Tip	80 pts
Eq 3rd	G L Jolly	Moroko Moon	78 pts
	R Dodge	Dodge's Paddington	78 pts

Champion of Champions Trophy: G L Jolly with Moorland Blaze, 88 pts

1980

NATIONAL CHAMPIONSHIPS

Open Judge: R Hutching

1st	G L Jolly	Moorland Blaxe	164 pts
2nd	G L Jolly	Blue Bush Magpie	161 pts
3rd	G L Jolly	Moorland Gem	130 pts

Improvers

1st	G L Jolly	Blue Bush Magpie	83 pts
Eq 2nd	G L Jolly	Moroko Doc	74 pts
	L Clifford	Le Cliff	
		Gentle Ben	74 pts

Maiden Judge: B Bashford

1st	R Dodge	Blue Bush Laddie	171 pts
2nd	G L Jolly	Moroko Peach	162 pts
3rd	G L Jolly	Moroko Doc	160 pts

ARNOTTS SPILLER'S CHAMPIONSHIPS

Open

1st	A N Scott	Miller's Fantastic	91 pts
2nd	R Dodge	Kenton Bill	88 pts
Eq 3rd	G L Jolly	Austral Blaze	86 pts
	A N Scott	Paroo Rad	86 pts

Improvers

1st	G L Jolly	Blue Bush Magpie	83 pts
Eq 2nd	L Clifford	Le Cliff	
		Gentle Ben	74 pts
	G L Jolly	Moroko Doc	74 pts

Maiden

1st	R Dodge	Blue Bush Laddie	92 pts
2nd	G L Jolly	Moroko Doc	84 pts
3rd	A N Scott	Moroko Happy	81 pts

Champion of Champions Trophy: R Dodge with Kenton Bill, 88 pts.

1981

Open   Judge: D Smith

1st	R Dodge	Kenton Bil	190 pts
2nd	L Noble	Tungali Tip	188 pts
3rd	A N Scott	Moroko Happy	187 pts

Improvers

1st	J Lawton	Stockman Topsy	182 pts
2nd	A N Scott	Moroko Happy	170 pts
3rd	J McIntosh	McIntosh's Jill	162 pts

Maiden   Judge: Mr D Carr

1st	R Dodge	Blue Bush Spook	180 pts
2nd	R Dodge	Penmore Dell	153 pts
3rd	D Smith	Barrackdale Boy	91 pts

ARNOTTS SPILLER'S CHAMPIONSHIPS

Open

1st	L Noble	Tungali Tip	95 pts
Eq 2nd	R Dodge	Kenton Bill	94 pts
	L Noble	Tungali Judy	94 pts

Improvers

1st	A N Scott	Moroko Happy	170 pts
2nd	J McIntosh	McIntosh's Jill	162 pts
3rd	J Lawton	Stockman Toss	89 pts

Maiden

1st	D Smith	Barrackdale Roy	91 pts
Eq 2nd	R Dodge	Penmore Dell	87 pts
	L Armstrong	Alphadale Mark	87 pts

Champion of Champions Trophy: R Smith with Quarrell's Biddy, 84 pts

1982

Open   Judge: J Elliott

1st	R Dodge	Whalam Sam	173 pts
Eq 2nd	M Semmens	Firrhill Jane	166 pts
	G L Jolly	Moorland Butch	166 pts

Improvers

1st	G L Jolly	Moorland Butch	172 pts
2nd	R Dodge	Viewfield Gypsy	165 pts
3rd	G L Jolly	Moroko Joe	160 pts

Maiden	Judge: A N Scott		
1st	R Dodge	Viewfield Gypsy	177 pts
2nd	T Percival	Doughty's Sam	146 pts
3rd	G L Jolly	Moorland Butch	93 pts

ARNOTTS SPILLER'S CHAMPIONSHIPS

Open			
1st	R Dodge	Whalam Sam	92 pts
Eq 2nd	L Armstrong	Alphadale Jill	90 pts
	G L Jolly	Moroko Joe	90 pts

Improvers			
1st	G L Jolly	Moroko Joe	90 pts
2nd	G L Jolly	Moorland Butch	88 pts
Eq 3rd	R Dodge	Viewfield Gypsy	85 pts
	M Semmens	Firrhill Jane	85 pts

Maiden			
1st	G L Jolly	Moorland Butch	93 pts
2nd	G L Jolly	Moroko Jay	89 pts
Eq 3rd	T Percival	Doughty's Sam	88 pts
	R Dodge	Viewfield Gypsy	88 pts

Champion of Champions Trophy: R Dodge with **Whalam Sam, 92 pts**

1983

NATIONAL CHAMPIONSHIPS

Open	Judge: B Bashford		
1st	W Carr	Tipp	165 pts
2nd	L Armstrong	Alphadale Kelly	162 pts
3rd	R Dodge	Dodge's Scout	161 pts

Improvers			
1st	R Dodge	Dodge's Scout	163 pts
2nd	J Dodge	Viewfield Gypsy	155 pts
3rd	W Carr	Hamilton's Gift	117 pts

Maiden	Judge: L Armstrong		
1st	R Seabrook	Marlowe Joe	159 pts
2nd	R Dodge	Kinton Tiger	156 pts
3rd	T Beard	Tomell Pete	148 pts

ARNOTTS HARPER CHAMPIONSHIPS

Open			
1st	R Dodge	Dodge's Scout	96 pts
2nd	D Smith	Borderview Pride	85 pts
3rd	L Armstrong	Alphadale Kelly	83 pts

170

Improvers

1st	R Dodge	Dodge's Scout	96 pts
2nd	W Carr	Penmore Mint	80 pts
Eq 3rd	J Dodge	Viewfield Gypsy	73 pts
	W Carr	Hamilton's Gift	73 pts

Maiden

1st	R Seabrook	Marlowe Joe	87 pts
2nd	C Camin	Rosemont Louise	86 pts
3rd	R Dodge	Kinton Tiger	83 pts

Champion of Champions Trophy: D Smith with Borderview Pride, 85 pts.

1984-87

Records Lost

1988

BICENTENNIAL CHAMPIONSHIP

Judge: B Bromham

1st	L E Noble	Sorrego Joe	84-73=157 pts
2nd	P T Slade	Glensloy Jock	77-disqualified=77
Eq 3rd	H Berry	Baluna Slade	72-retired=72 pts
	E A Gaby	Bengeo Jay	72-disqualified=72 pts

NATIONAL CHAMPIONSHIPS

Open   Judge: B Bonham

1st	E A Gaby	Bengeo Jay	93-969=162 pts
2nd	G J Prince	Wai Kiwki Coy	91-66=157 pts
3rd	L E Noble	Sorrego Joe	92-63=155 pts

Improver   Judge: B Bonham

1st	R Dodge	Bettmore Freckles	93-84=177 pts
2nd	R Dodge	Dodge's Ghandi	89-71=160 pts
3rd	L E Noble	Sorrego Joe	92-62=154 pts

Maiden   Judge: J Verena

1st	J H McDonald	Moorlands Mack	78-72=150 pts
2nd	W Carr	Typhoon Noble	78-48=126 pts
3rd	L M Walsh	Leerose Fantastic	78-41=119 pts

SKIPPA WORKING DOG CHAMPIONSHIPS

Open   Judge: B Bonham

Eq. 1st	E A Gaby	Bengeo Jay	93 pts
	R Dodge	Bettmore Freckles	93 pts
	P T Slade	Glensloy Jock	93 pts

Improver Judge: B Bonham
1st   R Dodge   Bettmore Freckles 93 pts
2nd   L E Noble   Sorrego Joe   92 pts
3rd   R Dodge   Dodge's Ghandi   89 pts

Maiden Judge: J Varena
1st   W L Slater   Wandarra Cloudy   85 pts
2nd   D Hines   Tarcoola Sheba   79 pts
Eq. 3rd   L Walsh   Leerose Fantastic 78 pts
            J H McDonald   Moorlands Mack   78 pts
            WE Carr   Typhoon Noble   78 pts

Champion of Champions Trophy: R Dodge with Quarrell's Bazza, 89 pts.

1989

NATIONAL CHAMPIONSHIPS

Open Judge: T Lindsay.
1st   L E Noble   Sorrego Bicie   91-89=180 pts
2nd   R Dodge   Viewfield Bess   89-77 pts
3rd   G J Prince   Rosedale Lady   90-75=165 pts

Improver Judge: T Lindsay
1st   A H Elliott   Gundagai Nimbo   76-67=146 pts
2nd   J McDonald   Moorlands Mack   79 pts
3rd   L Walsh   Leerose Hostess   77 pts

Maiden Judge: R Seabrook
1st   N J Webb   Hudson's Jemma   79-74=153 pts
2nd   G T Lindsay   Dodge's Sheedy   81-66=147 pts
3rd   A H Elliott   Gundagai Gemma   78-64=142 pts

SKIPPA WORKING DOG TRIAL

Open
1st   J Perry   Bengeo Speck   93 pts
Eq. 2nd   D. P Wilson   Tungali Kate   91 pts
            L E Noble   Sorrego Bicie   91 pts

Improver
Eq. 1st   A H Elliott   Gundagai Nimbo   79 pts
            J McDonald   Moorlands Mack   79 pts
3rd   L Walsh   Leerose Hostess   77 pts

Maiden
1st   G T Lindsay   Dodge's Sheedy   81 pts
Eq. 2nd   N. J. Webb   Hudson's Gemma   79 pts
            W Carr   Alroy Spring   79 pts

Champion of Champions Trophy: R Dodge with Viewfield Bess, 89 pts

172

1990

Open

1st	G. Prince	Rosedale Lady	85–84=172 pts
2nd	D Connop	Mirna Whisko	89–82=171 pts
3rd	N Webb	Glen Romian Kinte	86–84=170 pts

Improvers

1st	R Dodge	Patch	143 pts
2nd	J Perry	Wondara Grace	138 pts
3rd	G King	McIntosh's Midge	73 pts

Maiden

1st	R Dodge	Moynella Tip	175 pts
2nd	V Carr	Alroy Cap	167 pts
3rd	R Seabrook	Marlow Major	155 pts